Thomas Dykes

The Christian Church in Relation to Human Experience

A treatise on some ecclesiastical subjects, viewed chiefly with reference to the facts

of human nature and history

Thomas Dykes

The Christian Church in Relation to Human Experience
A treatise on some ecclesiastical subjects, viewed chiefly with reference to the facts of human nature and history

ISBN/EAN: 9783337164522

Printed in Europe, USA, Canada, Australia, Japan

Cover: Foto ©Lupo / pixelio.de

More available books at **www.hansebooks.com**

THE CHRISTIAN CHURCH

IN RELATION TO

HUMAN EXPERIENCE.

PUBLISHED BY
JAMES MACLEHOSE AND SONS, GLASGOW.

MACMILLAN AND CO., LONDON AND NEW YORK.
London, ... *Hamilton, Adams and Co.*
Cambridge, . . . *Macmillan and Bowes.*
Edinburgh, . . . *Douglas and Foulis.*

MDCCCLXXXV.

THE CHRISTIAN CHURCH

IN RELATION TO

HUMAN EXPERIENCE:

A TREATISE ON SOME ECCLESIASTICAL SUBJECTS, VIEWED CHIEFLY WITH REFERENCE TO THE FACTS OF HUMAN NATURE AND HISTORY.

BY

THOMAS DYKES, D.D.

GLASGOW:
JAMES MACLEHOSE & SONS,
Publishers to the University.
1885.

PREFACE.

THE history of ecclesiastical opinion is largely that of the maintenance of certain theories. The aim of the ecclesiastic has very generally been, not so much to ascertain what is in conformity with the wants and experience of man, as to uphold this or the other church-system. There is now, however, a considerable change of opinion in this respect. The view is widely and increasingly held that matters belonging to the outward manifestation of the religious life are to be considered rather in the light of their adaptation to actual circumstances than in accordance with theories. Instead of the belief, which was formerly prevalent, that all things relating to the Christian Church have been fixed by express divine appointment, it is a growing conviction that ecclesiastical matters are to be judged of by their tendency to fulfil the practical ends of religion, and to promote the good of man.

That this view of the principle which should be applied to the determination of church questions is the true one is attempted to be shown in some of the following pages. It is here mentioned, because it serves to explain the mode of treatment which has been employed in reference to the subjects which are discussed in this work. The purpose of the writer has been to consider these subjects mainly in relation to human nature and human experience. For this reason, the facts and views which belong to the past times of the Church's history have, so far as this could be done, been referred to. Ecclesiastical questions and difficulties form no exception to the truth of the wise man's saying, "The thing that hath been, it is that which shall be." The same problems which arise for solution in the present have been dealt with in the past. The tendencies which now run their course in the Christian Church, and produce certain effects, have appeared before, and with precisely the same results. The forms of ecclesiastical corrup-

Preface. vii

tion or error, which characterize the existing state of Christianity, have been substantially manifested in previous ages. It is obvious, therefore, that the most reliable grounds for forming a judgment in regard to points connected with the Church are furnished by a careful attention to the opinions and experiences of former periods of history.

The writer is indeed aware that elements of considerable difficulty are involved in not a few of the points which he has discussed, and that, notwithstanding all that may be said on them, their determination must be left in large measure to the exercise of enlightened judgment; but he hopes that the following contributions to the study of some important ecclesiastical subjects may have the effect of putting some things in a clearer light, and of affording aid to those desirous of arriving at just conclusions.

Ayr, May, 1885.

CONTENTS.

CHAPTER I.
THE UNITY OF THE CHURCH, - - - - 3

CHAPTER II.
SACERDOTALISM AND PURITANISM, - - - 41

CHAPTER III.
THE SCRIPTURES AND ECCLESIASTICAL MATTERS, - 81

CHAPTER IV.
CHANGE AS AN ELEMENT IN THE CHRISTIAN CHURCH, 121

CHAPTER V.
WORDS AND PHRASES CONNECTED WITH THE CHURCH, 157

CHAPTER VI.

CREEDS, - - - - - - - - 197

CHAPTER VII.

THE PURITY OF THE CHURCH, - - - - 235

CHAPTER VIII.

CONCLUSION, - - - - - - - 271

THE CHRISTIAN CHURCH

IN RELATION TO

HUMAN EXPERIENCE.

CHAPTER I.

THE UNITY OF THE CHURCH.

"It is good we return unto the ancient bounds of unity in the Church of God, which was one faith, one baptism; and not one hierarchy, one discipline."—LORD BACON.

THE UNITY OF THE CHURCH.

THE prayer of Christ in regard to His followers that they all might be one, and the various references in the New Testament to the unity of the Church, are very often understood as implying that Christians are intended to be united in one system of ecclesiastical polity. It is believed by those who take this view that the fact that there are differences among Christians as regards their modes of government and worship is in direct opposition to the will of Christ. That such a state of things exists is due, they hold, entirely to the sinfulness of human nature. Christ, it is argued, has authorized one, and only one, system of church-order; but men, in their wilfulness and perversity, have in many instances forsaken the only divine ecclesiastical *Common view of Christian unity.*

fold; and never, until they return to it, can the unity of the Church be realized.

Its impracticability.

When, however, the question is asked, *which* system of ecclesiastical order is it that Christ has sanctioned by His authority? to *what* form of church polity does He give His exclusive approval? we find that those who maintain the opinion that a uniform mode of government and ritual is binding on all Christians are hopelessly at variance. While the uncompromising upholder of Episcopacy tells us that the saving influences of religion are to be enjoyed only under the ministration of duly ordained bishops, the Presbyterian and Congregationalist have often insisted quite as strongly on the exclusive title of their respective forms of government to the favour of Heaven. Throughout all the divisions and subdivisions which separate Christians ecclesiastically, the same high ground has been assumed by every party in turn. For every mode of religious organization it has been contended that it, and it alone, is the type of polity which possesses the divine sanction, and to which, therefore, all believers in Christ are bound to conform.

Amidst this conflict of claims in support of the various forms of Church government, it has been, on the other hand, maintained by not a few that the controversy involves essential mistake; that there is, in point of fact, no one mode of ecclesiastical polity invested with the authority of Christ, but that men may differ in their judgment on this subject without transgressing any Christian law. Those who hold this opinion take the view which was expressed by one who, after hearing a debate on the question whether Presbytery or Episcopacy is the only divinely authorized system, remarked that, in his judgment, both sides claimed what neither possessed.[1] It is unreasonable to expect, say the maintainers of this view, that all Christians throughout the world should hold precisely the same forms of government and ritual. In no other department

The other view.

---

[1] "In the beginning of 1645, commissioners from the king (Charles I) met commissioners from the parliament at Uxbridge, to try if it were possible to arrange a peace. The competing claims of Episcopacy and Presbytery to a divine right were debated till the nobles were heartily tired; and the Marquis of Hertford put an end to the squabble by remarking that both claimed what he believed neither possessed." Cunningham's Church History of Scotland, vol. II. chap. iv.

of social life is rigid uniformity regarded as essential. There is no such thing in the ordinary experience of the world as unity without a large measure of external variety. When men associate for the maintenance of any object of common interest, they have their individual preferences as to the means which should be employed, and the modes in which expression should be given to their design. Varieties of temperament, differences of intellectual tendency, local influences, and such causes of diversified opinion, are so fully recognized in the ordinary relations of society that no one imagines that he will find in the sphere of common life exact identity of sentiment. We cannot with reason expect, it is argued, that it should be otherwise as regards *religious* matters, and that there should be absolute uniformity of judgment and usage in respect to *them*, any more than with reference to other subjects.

This the only view consistent with human nature.
While this, as it seems to us, is the only view consistent either with Scripture or with reason, and while we believe that those who maintain that there is only one type of church polity, to which all Christians must adhere, advocate a

doctrine opposed to the teachings of Christianity and the conditions of human nature, we by no means assert that all the differences which prevail in reference to ecclesiastical matters are justifiable. On the contrary, there can be no doubt that human sinfulness has had much to do with them. The influence of party spirit, and of extreme and unreasonable notions, has had a large share in producing the divisions which exist among Christian people. But, admitting this, it is a great mistake to ignore the fact that there are, independently altogether of such causes, those natural diversities of taste and disposition which make it impossible that the same mode of polity or worship can be suitable to all minds. As men are not cast in the same spiritual mould, nor exposed to the influence of the same circumstances and habits, there are sources of diversity which cannot but operate in reference to religion, quite apart from the differences that are traceable to infirmity of character.

In saying that the unity of the Christian Church can be rationally understood only when we regard it as consistent with a large measure *True religious unity presupposes voluntariness.*

of variety in matters of form and detail, it is of course presupposed that Christians are left free from external constraint; for it is a necessary condition of all real unity that it should be voluntary. The forcible exercise of outward authority, or the influence of spiritual despotism, may have sufficient power within the circle over which they rule to suppress liberty of thought, and by this means to create an almost entire sameness of religious belief and form. But this is not religious unity in the true sense of the term. Christians cannot be made "one" in the sense in which Christ intended His followers to be one, by surrendering their right to think, and giving themselves up blindly to the control of a human authority, who dictates to them whatever they are to believe and do. The effect, no doubt, when a multitude of persons all agree to accept such an authority as an absolute guide, is to produce identity of opinion. But it is identity of opinion arising from the fact that they do not exercise their own judgment. When the Church of Rome points to the unity which binds her communion together as presenting a contrast to the condition of Protestantism, the obvious reply is that a Church which prevents the exercise of freedom of thought among her members must always be more united after a sort than a religious society which permits inquiry and discussion; but that the agreement which is brought about by such means is not true unity. If concord is secured at the expense of mental life and freedom, it is the reverse of a benefit. Division of opinion is infinitely better than extinction of spiritual liberty.

The principle, then, for which we contend as furnishing the true idea of Christian unity is that of agreement as regards all that is essential in religion; while, on the other hand, many and wide differences must be expected among Christian people as respects non-essential matters. And in the latter class must be placed distinctions which relate to forms of government and worship. Questions connected with these subjects have been, and often are, discussed with as much keenness as if the existence of Christianity depended on them. But there can be no mistake more subversive of the true design of Christianity than to confound with the essence of faith and truth those things which have to do merely with

Therefore diversity inevitable even where there is substantial agreement.

external order. Nothing, perhaps, was ever more forcibly and truly expressed on this subject than the following words which were written by one who lived amidst the fierce ecclesiastical strife of the seventeenth century, but whose statement is not inapplicable to later times:—"As for the Popish clergymen, hold what you will, if you hold not the supremacy of the Pope, all the rest of your religion is not worth a rush. Come to the Episcopal clergy; if you acknowledge not episcopal government, if you submit not to the liturgy, and ceremonies, and vestments, and music used in the Church, you are at best a schismatic. Again, come to the Presbyterian clergy; they will tell you that episcopal government is Romish and superstitious, and their ceremonies and usages anti-christian usurpation; but, if you mean to be of a warrantable religion, you must submit to the presbyterian government as truly apostolical. Come to the Independent; he declaims against both the former, and tells you that the true conformity to apostolical order is the congregational way. Take the Anabaptist; and he tells you that all the former are vain and irreligious, unless you will be rebaptized and

A statement regarding ecclesiastical differences.

listed in his Church. It is a pitiful thing to see men run upon this mistake. Every man measures the religion or irreligion of another by their agreeing or dissenting with them in these or the like matters; and at best, while we scramble and wrangle about the pieces of the shell, the kernel is lost. Believe it, religion is quite another thing from all these matters. He that fears the Lord of heaven and earth, walks humbly before Him, thankfully lays hold of the message of redemption by Christ Jesus, strives to express his thankfulness by the sincerity of his obedience, is true in his promise, just in his actions, charitable to the poor, sincere in his devotions, that will not deliberately dishonour God, that hath his hope in heaven, and his conversation in heaven: such a man, whether he be an Episcopalian, or a Presbyterian, or an Independent, or an Anabaptist; whether he wears a surplice, or wears none; whether he hears organs, or hears none; whether he kneels at the communion, or for conscience' sake stands, or sits, *he* hath the life of religion in him. On the other side, if a man fears not the eternal God, dares commit any sin with presumption, can drink excessively, swear vainly or falsely, commit adultery, lie, cheat, break his promises, live loosely; though he practise every ceremony never so curiously, or as stubbornly oppose them; though he cry down bishops, or cry down presbytery; though he be rebaptized every day, or declaim against it as heresy; though he fast all the Lent, or feast out of pretence of avoiding superstition, yet, notwithstanding all these, he wants the life of religion."[1]

Strong reasons for latitude in church matters.

In his preface to this testimony, Richard Baxter tells us, from personal knowledge of its author, that he preferred episcopacy before all other forms of church government, but without superstitious attachment to it. The truth is that the sentiments expressed in the above words are only such as those who hold moderate ecclesiastical views may consistently subscribe to, whatever

---

[1] The Judgement of the late Lord Chief Justice, Sir Matthew Hale, of the Nature of True Religion, the Causes of its Corruption, and the Churches' calamity, by Men's Additions and Violences, with the Desired Cure. Humbly dedicated to the Honourable Judges, and Learned Lawyers, who knew and honoured the Author, by the faithful publisher Richard Baxter. London, 1684. Printed for B. Simmons, at the Three Cocks, near the West End of St. Paul's Church.

their personal preferences in respect of church polity. While one holds that this or the other form of ecclesiastical government or worship is, for him at least, the best, there is no reason why he should insist on its being the only form to be adopted by others. There are the strongest possible reasons for the widest latitude in regard to these matters. They do not involve the substance of Christianity. Unity in everything that is fundamental in religion may co-exist with a large measure of variety in the external details of order and ritual; and any attempt that can be made to prevent the divergent tendencies of human nature from having reasonable scope in respect to such things can only end in injury to religion itself. And, while the history of the Christian Church presents us with a terrible record of conflict between opposing ecclesiastical parties; Prelate and Presbyter, Nonconformist and Churchman, and supporters of each various system, denouncing as fatally in error those who differ from them; there have always been, as we have said, men adhering to the different modes of polity, who, like the writer whom we have quoted, have pled for wider views,—who have urged that, in relation to matters of form, and of subordinate importance, there ought to be every allowance in the Church of Christ for diversity of opinion. It was to this liberal view that the judgment of the Protestant Reformers consistently led, imperfectly as they sometimes carried out its spirit.[1] It is the opinion set forth by Lord Bacon as the fruit of lengthened study of Scripture.[2] The greatest English writer on ecclesiastical polity supplies, as we shall afterwards see, when we come to treat of his opinions, much powerful argument in support of liberty in matters of church order.[3] Richard Baxter sought to unite the contending ecclesiastical parties of his day on a basis of mutual toleration. Archbishop Leighton, who also vainly attempted the same task in a different sphere, expressed the guiding principle of his life in the words —" The mode of church govern-

This an opinion supported by many of all parties.

---

[1] The opinions of the leading Reformers in regard to the grounds of ecclesiastical polity will be found in Chapter III.

[2] The Pacification of the Church of England. The passage is quoted in Chapter III.

[3] Hooker's Laws of Ecclesiastical Polity. His views as bearing on the foundation of ecclesiastical order, will also be found in Chapter III.

ment is immaterial; but peace and concord, kindness and goodwill are indispensable."[1] The leading Independents of the time of the Commonwealth advocated latitude in regard to church matters. "I hope for a time," says John Howe, "when Christianity will be the religion of the world. While it is cramped, it will never grow. I do not hope it will prevail in the world by having all the world reduced to the model of this or that party. How absurdly arrogant would he be that should pray that all the world might be of one mind by being all brought to be precisely of *his* mind! When I see truly catholic Christianity coming into repute; when the great things of religion do more engage men's minds, and they cease to magnify trifles; when the love of God comes to govern the Christian Church, and reign in the hearts of men; then will the Kingdom of God come with power."[2]

Such are some instances — instances which might easily be multiplied — of prominent and thoughtful men belonging to different ecclesiasti-

[1] Pearson's Life of Archbishop Leighton.
[2] Some Consideration of a Preface to an Enquiry concerning the Occasional Conformity of Dissenters.

cal parties, who have been ready to recognize the principle of freedom as an element of true religious unity.

<small>Teaching of Scripture on the subject.</small> The question which has next to be considered is, how far this view accords with the representations of Scripture on the subject of the unity of the Church? Now, when we refer to the teachings of Christ himself, we find that he never enjoins any one form of ecclesiastical government, or any fixed mode of worship, as the means of securing unity among his followers. His prayer in behalf of those who believe in Him, that "they all may be one, as Thou, Father, art in Me, and I in Thee, that they also may be one in Us; that the world may believe that Thou hast sent Me,"[1] manifestly contemplates a spiritual, rather than a formal, bond of union. It is a prayer which far transcends the mere outward and mechanical conception of unity. The nature of the agreement to which it refers is such as consists in mutual love, and in fellowship of spirit and character.[2] Nor

---

[1] John xvii. 21.

[2] As regards our Lord's declaration in John x. 16, which is given in the Authorized Version as, "There shall be one fold, and one shepherd," an important change is made by the true translation, which is supplied by the

are the statements of the Apostles on the subject of Christian unity less clearly distinguished by the same large and spiritual views. In those figurative representations which they employ to illustrate this subject; in which the Church is compared to a building joined together by the connection of its various parts with one foundation,[1] to a body the members of which are united by a common principle of life,[2] to a family of which God is the Father;[3] the meaning evidently intended to be conveyed is that all Christians are one in virtue of their vital relationship to Christ. That is the view which these representations give of the unity of Christians; and not that it consists in their being combined in a uniform system of organization. And, moreover, the spirituality of the terms which are constantly used in the Apostolic writings, when the subject of the union of believers in Christ is spoken of, emphatically indicates the same thing. Thus the unity which

Revised Version—"They shall become one *flock*, one shepherd." What is meant, says Alford, is "not one fold, but one flock; no one exclusive enclosure of an outward Church, but one flock, all knowing the one Shepherd, and known of Him."

[1] Eph. ii. 20; 1 Pet. ii. 4.　　[2] 1 Cor. xii. 12; Col. ii. 19.
[3] Eph. ii. 19; Gal. vi. 10.

B

Christians are exhorted to keep is described as "unity of the Spirit,"[1] and as "the unity of the faith and of the knowledge of the Son of God."[2] "In one Spirit," it is said, "were we all baptised into one body, and were all made to drink of one Spirit."[3] "Ye are all one," it is also declared, "in Christ Jesus."[4] When St. Paul particularizes the elements which he regards as constituting the unity of Christians, he does not represent uniformity of external order and government as the bond of connection. His words have a much more wide and comprehensive scope. He says: "There is one body, and one Spirit, even as also ye were called in one hope of your calling; one Lord, one faith, one baptism, one God and Father of all, who is over all, and through all, and in all."[5]

The testimony of Scripture adverse to confining religion to a single outward type.

We are very far from arguing that the teaching of Christ and the Apostles affords any encouragement to the view of those who are inclined to disparage the importance of the external institutions and ordinances of the Christian Church. So far as these minister to the

[1] Eph. iv. 3.   [2] Eph. iv. 13.   [3] 1 Cor. xii. 13.
[4] Gal. iii. 28.   [5] Eph. iv. 4-6.

preservation of the order and seemliness which should characterize Christian work and worship, they fulfil an office of essential moment. We cannot do without government and discipline in the Church any more than we can dispense with them in the regulation of the every-day affairs of social life. But our argument from the teaching of Christ and the Apostles is, that it is opposed to the ecclesiastical exclusiveness that would confine religion to one type of polity. It gives supreme prominence to the spiritual and moral elements of religion, and not to the outward mode in which these are manifested. It inculcates as all-important that men should believe the truth and live a Christian life, while to external matters it assigns a place altogether subordinate. "The holy Church throughout all the world" is not, according to the descriptions of the New Testament, this or the other outward organization. Its distinguishing features are faith, and love, and goodness. Where these exist Christianity exists, whatever may be the ecclesiastical distinctions with which it is connected. And thus, important as external systems and institutions are, the Scriptural idea of the Christian society is wider than any of them. It is wide enough to embrace all faithful servants of Christ everywhere.

<small>Protestantism also adverse to one exclusive type of polity.</small>

It may be justly claimed for this view of the unity of the Christian Church, which is opposed to identifying it exclusively with any special form of ecclesiastical order, that it alone is in accordance with the principle of spiritual freedom asserted in Protestantism. For, if liberty of judgment in matters of religion is to be allowed for as an element in the existence of the Christian Church, it is manifest that diversity must be expected in the modes in which ecclesiastical life is developed. It is inconsistent and absurd to suppose that men are to exercise freedom of thought and conscience, and, at the same time, are to be confined within the limits of a uniform system. Religious liberty cannot be had without varieties of religious form. The Reformers themselves realized this only in part. It happened with them, as commonly happens with men who bring newly to light a truth which is generally unrecognized. They saw clearly enough the unspeakable value of religious liberty; but they failed to apprehend with equal clearness the results which their claim to its possession legitimately involved. They looked at it from the point of view of their relation to the Church of Rome, without sufficiently remembering that it had a much more general bearing,—that the freedom of judgment which Protestants contended for in relation to that Church, they were also bound to concede to it, and to each other. But, however much of failure there was practically on the part of the Reformers to maintain the liberality of view in regard to ecclesiastical matters, which was the proper result of their position, the early confessions of Protestantism express conceptions of the Church of Christ which are characterized by great breadth and spirituality. The following are some of their representations—" The Church is the congregation of saints, the assembly of all believers, in which the gospel is rightly taught, and the sacraments are rightly administered. And unto the true unity of the Church it is sufficient to agree concerning the gospel and the administration of the sacraments. Nor is it necessary that human traditions, rites, or ceremonies instituted by man should be alike everywhere; as St. Paul

Testimony of the early Protestant Confessions.

saith, There is one faith, one baptism, one God and Father of all."[1] "The Church is not merely a society of external matters and ceremonies, like other communities; but it is chiefly a society of faith, and of the Holy Spirit in the hearts of men; which, however, has outward marks by which it can be recognized, namely, the pure teaching of the gospel, and the administration of the sacraments in accordance with the gospel of Christ."[2] "We believe in one holy Christian Church, that is, the fellowship of the saints, the congregation of spiritual believers, which is holy, and the bride of Christ, in which all are citizens who confess truly that Jesus Christ is the Lamb of God, and approve that faith by works."[3] "We believe in one catholic or universal Church, which

---

[1] The Augsburg Confession, 1530. This confession was prepared by Melanchthon. In quoting from this and other creeds, both here and in subsequent chapters, reference has been made to the texts of Niemeyer, Winer, and Schaff.

[2] The Apology of the Augsburg Confession, 1530; also the work of Melanchthon.

[3] The Confession of Basle, 1534, which was among the earliest of the Swiss confessions, and was prepared by Œcolompadius and Myconius, who were associated with Zwingle in the Reformation movement.

is a holy congregation or assembly of all truly faithful Christians, who expect their whole salvation in Jesus Christ alone, having been washed in His blood, and sanctified and sealed through His Spirit. This holy Church is not situated or confined in a certain place, neither is it bound to certain and special persons, but is spread and diffused throughout the whole world; and yet is joined and united with heart and will by the power of faith in one and the same spirit."[1] "The truth and unity of the Church consists, not in ceremonies and external rites, but rather in the truth and unity of the catholic faith. The catholic faith has not been delivered to us in human laws, but in Divine Scripture, and its compendium is the Apostles' Creed."[2]

These truly catholic declarations of early Protestantism are in singular contrast to the condition of things which became prevalent later on in the history of Protestantism. At a later

Causes of the departure of Protestantism from its earliest views.

---

[1] The Belgic Confession, 1561. This was the original Protestant symbol of the Netherlands, and is still recognized by the Reformed Churches in Holland and Belgium.

[2] The Second Helvetic Confession, 1566; a Swiss confession of a somewhat later period than that of Basle; the work of Bullinger, the pupil, friend, and successor, of Zwingle.

period, as we have seen, so far from the Church being regarded as, in the language of the Apology for the Confession of Augsburg, "chiefly a society of faith and of the Holy Spirit in the hearts of men, and not of external matters," it was dealt with as involving questions of outward polity most of all. Supreme prominence came to be given to distinctions of form. The divine standing of a Christian society came to be discussed as depending mainly or entirely on the nature of its government and the ritual which it used. This growth of narrower views affords an instance of what is not at all exceptional in the history of religion. Wide and spiritual ideas of truth often become contracted with lapse of time. The effect of tradition frequently is to render more prominent the merely literal and outward elements of truth, while its living spirit is less and less regarded. But, while the change from the wider views, which were characteristic of the earliest age of Protestantism, to those contracted and exclusive notions of church matters that belong to a later time, is to be explained mainly by this general cause, there is also reason, we think, to connect it with a distinction which was introduced by Protestant theologians at an early date. We refer to the distinction between the Church "visible," and the Church "invisible." When understood in a certain sense these terms serve to indicate a fact relating to the Christian Church, which is of much practical importance.[1] The phraseology does not seem, however, very well-chosen, even for the purpose of representing this fact; and it is certainly liable to convey a false impression. For, when the Church of Christ, in the largest and fullest sense of the term,—the Church which includes all true servants of Christ, and whose bond of union is of a spiritual nature, consisting in faith and the Christian life,—is described as "invisible," the natural effect of the epithet is to convey the idea that it belongs to the region of dim abstraction, and has little or nothing to do with the practical purposes of religion. And, on the other hand, when the Church as an external organization, constituted of outward forms and ordinances, is designated as the "visible" em-

[1] The true and original sense of this distinction will be found in the remarks on ecclesiastical phraseology in Chapter V.

bodiment of religion, the equally natural result is to give the impression that it alone is of practical interest or importance. Such we believe to have been the false idea which this phraseology encouraged. It helped to bring the merely external matters of religion too prominently into the foreground, while it tended to depreciate its spiritual elements. Its tendency in this respect is precisely the opposite of what the representations of the New Testament convey. For these emphatically describe the Church of Christ as first of all, and supremely based on common principles of faith and righteousness; and only subordinately, and in a far inferior degree, as depending on external order. The language of the distinction to which we are referring has tended to foster an opinion the very reverse of this.

Prominence given to the dogma of the visible Church subsequent to the Reformation age.

It may be thought that, in attributing the production of those narrower views which became developed in the history of Protestantism to the influence, in some measure, of this phrase, we are assigning more than its due importance to the effect of a verbal distinction. It is, however, a historical fact that, in the age succeeding the

Reformation, the merely external conception of the Church gradually acquired a prominence which ended in its overshadowing those more wide and spiritual views which had been held in the earliest period of Protestantism; and that this departure connected itself with the importance given to the dogma of the "Visible Church." It became the all-absorbing ecclesiastical idea to establish a Kingdom of Christ on earth, which was to be the embodiment of religious truth and life—to set up a visible society of Christians, to which all believers in Christ must belong. Under the influence of this idea, such larger and more tolerant sentiments in regard to the Church as had been entertained at first receded into the background, and it became the great object with each ecclesiastical party to prove that *it* was the sole heaven-appointed communion. Hence the most narrow and exclusive claims were advanced on every side.

Let us now briefly recall the conclusions to which the preceding observations have led us regarding the unity of the Christian Church:—

We have, first of all, seen that the theory of Recapitulation.

Christian unity, which accepts it as essential that all Christians should be united in one external form of polity, is not in accordance with human nature. There are, we have endeavoured to point out, such marked diversities inherent in human nature that nothing else can reasonably be expected than that the religious life should assume a variety of outward modes. We have also argued that questions affecting ecclesiastical order and forms of worship, though they have been largely treated as if they are of transcendent importance, do not really belong to the essence of Christianity; and that, therefore, it is well that they should be judged of in a spirit of freedom, and that it should not be attempted to bind men down to uniformity in reference to them. This, we have shown, is the view which has been maintained by many leading men of different ecclesiastical parties. It has also been pointed out that the testimony of Scripture is in the same direction —that the idea of unity which Christ and the Apostles describe is not that of identity of polity and form, but that of fellowship in faith and righteousness. And we have argued further that the principle of spiritual liberty asserted in Protestantism is necessarily adverse to rigid uniformity in religious matters.

To the view of Christian unity, which we have thus endeavoured to advocate, an objection is made, which will now have to be considered. It is argued that the latitude which this view would give to diversities of opinion in religious things, and the non-essential character which it attributes to matters of church government and ritual, must tend to encourage division in the Christian Church. Once admit, it is said, that differences may exist as regards forms of ecclesiastical polity and external observances without any violation of the divine will, and you must be prepared to expect all sorts of religious separations to be defended as legitimate. But there is a two-fold answer to this objection. In the first place, no principle, however true in itself, can be secured against the possibility of abuse. The possession of freedom, whatever may be the sphere of human action in which it is enjoyed, will always lead, more or less, to extremes. And, therefore, it is not a just objection to the opinion of those who are in favour of latitude as respects church matters, to urge that it may be carried to excess.

Objection that foregoing view tends to encourage division.

But there is another and more conclusive reply to this objection. Instead of a liberal view of differences of Christian opinion tending to produce divisions in the Christian Church, it is from the opposite cause, in great measure, that separation and dissension have resulted. Those who have produced the worst excesses of ecclesiastical disunion are those who have insisted on an impracticable exactness of agreement, not those who have been disposed to allow freedom. The stern denouncer of all deviations from a single type of church polity as sinful is really—while he supposes that he is conserving the unity of the Church — doing the very thing which produces and embitters division. When the endeavour is made to limit religion within too narrow boundaries, and to deny to it that liberty to differ, which is but reasonable, the necessary result is to cause separation and conflict. Thus; to revert once more to a period in the history of the Church, which is memorable for the intensity of its ecclesiastical differences; the state of matters in the seventeenth century is strikingly illustrative of the tendency of too rigid notions of the unity of Christians to create division. The idea

Division largely produced by unreasonable opposition to religious differences.

of the age was that all Christians are bound to conform to one mode of church polity. There is but one ecclesiastical system, it was held, which has the divine sanction; and, unless men adhere to it, they are guilty of heinous sin. What was the effect? Not certainly to prevent religious divisions. The result, on the contrary, was to multiply them. The author of the "Liberty of Prophesying" gives us a picture of this age, which is coloured to a certain extent, no doubt, by satirical humour; but which may be taken, at the same time, as representing with only too much truth the religious condition of things. He describes 500 sects as all condemning each other—each one denouncing all the rest, and itself treated in the same manner by the remaining 499.[1] Thus it is that the narrowness which seeks to prevent the existence of differences within the limits of the Christian Church only leads to division and discord. And, on the other hand, nothing can tend more effectually to produce reasonableness and moderation in regard to the things in which

[1] Jeremy Taylor's Liberty of Prophesying. The Epistle Dedicatory.

Christians differ than the recognition of the fact that the existence of diversity of opinion is inevitable, and that there is room enough for it without sacrificing anything of essential unity.

<small>Advantages of an external ecclesiastical unity often greatly overrated.</small>
These observations serve to indicate in what direction a remedy is to be sought for the evils which are connected with ecclesiastical divisions. The cure lies rather in the growth of a spirit of moderation than in any re-arrangement of the outward conditions of Christianity. There are many who think that the greatest possible efforts should be made to bring men of different communions to abandon their position of separation from each other, and become united in one organization. Their view is that this would constitute, if it could be accomplished, the most desirable and delightful of all consummations. But the worth of a movement of this kind is often greatly overrated. The real value of an amalgamation of the divided elements of the ecclesiastical world depends mainly on the nature of the causes which bring it about. If it is the natural growth of larger and truer Christian feeling, and is produced by wider views and sympa-

thies, well and good. But, if it is the result of quite other causes, if it arises from motives which partake rather of policy than of Christianity, it can hardly be said to be a gain to the interests of religion. Schemes of ecclesiastical comprehension have been often tried, but they have not yielded the fruits which were expected by their enthusiastic supporters. The principle involved in them is not one that is adequate to meet the state of the case. For the mere external unification of Christians—unification which does not arise from the religious spirit, but is due to agencies and influences operating from without —instead of being of service to the promotion of Christianity, may be the reverse. It may be attended with effects more undesirable than the separations which it professes to heal; because it involves other motives than those by which Christian union should be inspired. Therefore, there is reason, we think, to look with much distrust on all artificial projects and arrangements for doing away with ecclesiastical disunion, and effecting a combination of the separate sections of the Christian Church. Any spontaneous movement towards the manifestation of a freer and larger religious spirit is of value; but not an artificially-created unity.

<small>Diversity of parties attended with good as well as evil.</small> Besides, it should be remembered that the differences which exist in the Christian world are far from being an unqualified evil. While there are acknowledged elements of sin attendant on the separations which prevail in the Church, there is a considerable element of good mingled with them. The interests of truth are promoted by diversity of views. This is overlooked by those who imagine that, if only Christians could become united in one external system of polity and belief, it would be an inestimable blessing. Unanimity and uniformity in matters of religion are not, in point of fact, the desirable things they are often taken to be. It is only when there is mental stagnation that there is absolute sameness of opinion. Wherever, on the contrary, there is spiritual life, distinctions of individual tendency and thought are certain to come prominently out. And, therefore, it is not to be wished, in the interests of intelligent and living Christianity, that there should be a cessation of the element of diversity in religious matters. However ardently it is to be

desired that the spirit of strife might be excluded from the Christian Church, variety of opinion and form is in itself beneficial. It tends ultimately in the direction of truer conviction and fuller life. We are dependent on differences of thought for the maintenance of healthful religious views, just as we are dependent on the same source for just and wise conclusions as regards the affairs of life generally.

And, on the other hand, it should also be borne in mind that, were all Christians united in one outward organization, it would not necessarily have the effect of removing that which is the great evil of disunion—party strife. Within a body externally united there may exist, and there often do exist, the worst forms of dissension. There are frequently far more opposition of sentiment and bitterness of feeling between those who are members of the same community than exist between separate communities. The ardent maintainer of the idea that the evils of Christendom are to be cured by the uniting of all Christians in one body, forgets this. He loses sight of the fact that beneath the surface of a union which is outward there may be the most discordant

External unity does not preclude dissension.

conditions. The use of the term "schism" by St. Paul affords a striking illustration of this fact. That term has come to be applied solely to the case of ecclesiastical separation, in conformity with the notion that an external unity of Christians fulfils the purpose of Christ in regard to His Church. But that is not the sense in which the Apostle makes use of the word. When he accused the Corinthian believers of "schism," he meant by it dissensions which existed internally in their communion.[1] This apostolic application of the word is important as showing that nothing may be gained, so far as the creation of real spiritual agreement is concerned, by the fact of Christians being combined in one outward society. That may be the actual state of things where there is an absence of true unity.

True Christian unity that of spirit, not of form. To look, therefore, on the mere union of Christians in one organization as satisfying the design of Christ, when He referred to the unity of His followers, is an entirely inadequate view of the subject. Nor is it less a misapprehension to suppose that the real unity of Christians involves

---

[1] Some observations on the apostolic use of the term "schism" are contained in Chapter V.

the extinction of diversities of opinion. We take a far higher and more reasonable view of the nature of that oneness which is designed to characterize the Christian Church, when we regard it as in no way superseding natural differences of temperament and tendency, but as being in full accordance with the manifestation of such differences. And the remedy to which this view points for the evils which are attendant on religious division, is, as we have said, the growth of a spirit of moderation and tolerance. Varieties of thought and of external system are by no means in themselves an evil; but, on the contrary, the most important services to the cause of truth are rendered by them. It is in the excesses with which diversity of opinion is accompanied, and the violence of feeling by which it is so often embittered, that the evil connected with it lies. Instead, therefore, of vainly endeavouring after a unity of the church which is to obliterate all distinctions, the truer and wiser view of the subject is to accept the element of variety as having its place and purpose in the sphere of religion. And, in thus claiming that Christianity is wide enough to embrace different views and phases of ecclesiastical order, we claim for it that it makes men one in the highest of all senses,— that its unity is unity with freedom,—that the oneness it seeks to create is that of spirit and life, not of form.

CHAPTER II.

SACERDOTALISM AND PURITANISM.

"They that are against superstition oftentimes run into it on the wrong side."—SELDEN.

SACERDOTALISM AND PURITANISM.

THE tendency to identify religion with lofty views of the clerical office and elaborate ceremonial has been manifested in every period of the history of the Church. On the other hand, there has been very frequently exhibited a tendency to the opposite extreme of excessive rigour as regards religious observances. The one movement has been characterized by fondness for ornate ritual, and the disposition to invest the ministerial office with attributes of mysterious spiritual power; the other by antipathy to ceremonies, and an austere abstinence from everything externally attractive in the service of God. We propose to consider some of the main features of these two forms of religious feeling. The opposite influences of Sacerdotalism and Puritanism have not only *Nature of the two extremes.*

entered largely into the ecclesiastical contests of the past, but they are still active ecclesiastical forces.

I.

The Sacerdotal view of religion—the view which is in the direction of assigning a priestly character to the Christian ministry and investing matters of ceremonial with extreme importance—while it is foreign to the spirit and teaching of the New Testament, is a form of opinion, the development of which out of primitive Christianity is distinctly traceable.

Rise and growth of sacerdotalism in early Christian times. In the primitive period of the history of the Christian Church, the office of the ministry was nothing more than that of religious overseer and teacher. Its position and functions were not regarded as involving mysterious elements of spiritual power. The language of the New Testament in reference to the Christian ministry does not suggest that there was anything essentially different in their standing from that of other Christians. On the contrary, it is the doctrine of the New Testament that Christ, by the sacrifice which He offered once for all, brought the Jewish ceremonies and priestly system to an end, and constituted all His followers, without exception, a spiritual priesthood.[1] But this moderate estimate of the position of the ministry gave place, as early as the close of the second century, to more elevated notions. The language which denotes priesthood—applied at first to the Christian minister without perhaps any intention of attributing extraordinary prerogatives to him—came to be used in its literal and sacrificial sense. The ministerial office became invested in common opinion, with a sacred and authoritative character, which raised it far above the sphere of the members of the Church. The ministry were increasingly regarded as forming a class essentially distinct from the Christian people. They were looked on as endowed with special divine power, and as the only appointed channel of saving grace. Side by side with these lofty ideas of the ministerial office there arose, as might be expected, increasing devotion to ceremonies and greater elaboration of the forms of religious worship. The simplicity which had

[1] 1 Peter ii. 5 ; Rev. i. 6.

characterized the ritual of the primitive age of the Church was superseded by a profuse external symbolism. Christian devotion lost in multiplied rites its original spirituality.[1]

Such was the process by which sacerdotalism rose into power in the early Christian centuries, and the result of that change is represented in the Church of Rome and the Greek Church, which are historically the development of the influences in the direction of priestly rule and ceremonial that characterized this epoch.

But, although this is the most extensive example in Christian history of the rise and growth of sacerdotal ideas, movements of essentially the same character have often occurred in the Christian Church. And one instance, in particular, is so important and so illustrative of the process to which we are referring that it may be also appropriately stated as exemplifying the development of sacerdotalism:—

Rise and growth of sacerdotalism in the Church of England.

The Reformation in England was attended by a return to the New Testament conception of the

[1] Dissertation on the Christian Ministry by Lightfoot (Bishop of Durham). Neander's Church History, vol. i. 244, etc. (Clark's Translation). Pressensé's Early Years of Christianity.

ministerial office as being nothing more than that of pastor and teacher. When the founders of the Church of England adopted the episcopal mode of government they chose it as the best and wisest system of church-order in the circumstances for which they were called to provide. But they had no exclusive views of church government, or of the Christian ministry. Cranmer, Ridley, Latimer, and the other representatives of English Episcopacy in its earliest age, had no faith in the divine right of bishops. They regarded the office of bishop as not originally different from that of presbyter. They were utterly hostile to all priestly claims on the part of the clergy. The basis, in short, on which the English Episcopal system was originally founded was moderate and liberal. Before the end of the reign of Elizabeth, however, the same tendency towards investing the clergy and the ritual of the Church with excessive importance began to manifest itself, which we have described as having characterized the period following the apostolic age. What have since become known as "high-church" views acquired increasing influence. The bishops of the Church of England possessed, it was now alleged, certain special elements of spiritual power and prerogative through derivation of their orders from the Apostles, while Presbyterian ordination began to be assailed as invalid. And, with the growth of these lofty views in reference to the position and functions of the clergy, there was a corresponding development of religious ceremonial. The rites of divine worship were multiplied, and were invested with increasing show. The result was that, when Archbishop Laud carried out to its consummation this change in the views and usages of the Church of England, it was almost entirely under the domination of sacerdotal ideas.[1]

The sacerdotal tendency has its foundation in human nature.

These instances from church-history show the nature of the sacerdotal tendency, as well as the fact that it belongs to the common susceptibilities of religious feeling. The disposition to attribute to the clergy extraordinary spiritual authority and power, and to assign pre-eminent importance to ceremonial, is evidently—however we may account

---

[1] Hallam's Constitutional History of England, Chapters ii., iv., and vii. Hunt's Religious Thought in England, Chapters i. ii.

for it—a deeply-rooted propensity of human nature. The two examples which we have given were both departures from pre-existing views; the priestly systems of the Greek and Roman Churches having little in common with the primitive conceptions of Christianity, to which they succeeded; while the transcendental claims of Anglicanism are an entire change from the opinions of the founders of the Church of England. But the very circumstance that such departures occurred; the very fact of the disposition towards priestly ideas of religion being strong enough to establish itself in opposition to existing modes of belief; is itself a striking testimony to the power of this feeling. It shows clearly that there must be strong elements of support and encouragement in human nature for the priestly view of the ministry and of divine worship. And any one who looks at the state of Christendom generally, and contemplates the extent to which it is under the influence of such forms of faith and devotion as make a human priesthood the centre of religion, must arrive at the same conclusion.

The question then arises, To what causes are we to trace the prevalence of sacerdotalism?

External causes which led to its development.

Now, it is undeniable that, as in most cases in which change of opinion is introduced and developed, external circumstances have had to do with the rise and growth of this phase of religion. Thus, when we revert to the post-apostolic period in the history of the Christian Church, it is obvious that the outward influences amidst which Christianity existed in that age were strongly in favour of excessive ceremonialism, as well as exaggerated views of the office of the ministry. The system of Judaism, though properly belonging to a state of things which had passed away, continued still to leaven the institutions of Christianity. St. Paul had foreseen the evils which were likely to arise from the Judaizing element, and had striven against it with the intense earnestness which was characteristic of his nature. But we know from the history of the early Christian era that this influence remained to mould, in no small degree, the ordinances of the Christian Church; and that Jewish ideas and rites passed over into the new system of faith. And, on the other hand, the elements of heathen superstition, amidst which Christianity was founded, were not less favourable to the growth of external usages in connection with the Church, which were entirely foreign to the spirituality of the gospel of Christ. From this source, as well as from Judaism, early Christianity became infected with false views in reference to the office of the ministry, and the nature and forms of religious worship. It is also apparent that the outward circumstances with which the existence of Protestantism was connected subsequent to the Reformation were such as powerfully tended towards the same result. Though the English Church had avowedly thrown off the system of Rome, the traditions of the past were still of sufficient influence to favour a reaction, and to make a return to the priestly ceremonialism of the older state of things a by no means unlikely event.

But, independently altogether of external influences, there are predisposing tendencies in human nature itself, which operate strongly in favour of sacerdotalism.

And, first of all, the belief that the ministers of religion are possessed of mysterious spiritual power, and that certain rites and forms convey supernatural influence, is in accordance with the *Causes of sacerdotalism in human nature. First, the disposition to a religion of outward observances*

D

disposition to regard religion as consisting in mere outward observances. This is one of the strongest and most widely prevailing tendencies of human feeling. There is always an inclination to trust for the favour of God to external means and powers, instead of assigning supreme importance to the condition of the heart and life. Hence a system which gives special prominence to ritual, and which holds forth to the worshipper the hope of obtaining divine grace through the extraordinary virtue of outward ordinances, is necessarily a system which possesses powerful attractions. It appeals to the fondness which a large class of persons have for the notion that religion operates as a sort of charm. To believe that there is an occult spiritual force exerted by the official attributes of the ministry, that certain forms have an inherent mysterious power to confer the favour of Heaven, and that within the sphere of some priestly influence the light of truth and the love of God are with certainty enjoyed, is to view Christian faith and devotion as having the nature of a mystic spell. And this very fact constitutes the reason of the gratification which is afforded by such a mode of religious belief. There is an obvious source of satisfaction in the thought that our relation to God is made right by ceremonial influences that act in some inscrutable fashion; and that, when we observe a certain ritual, and possess a certain order of ministry, we stand well for the world to come. Nor should it be overlooked that a system which thus assigns pre-eminent value to the merely outward elements of religion, draws much of the power with which it appeals to the sympathy of common opinion from the circumstance that it offers a comparatively easy solution of the requirements of Christian service. The great practical difficulty which Christianity involves is that it demands moral reformation, and a life of purity and good works, as its absolutely essential results. The teaching of the New Testament is emphatically to the effect that the only true manifestation of Christian earnestness lies in sanctity of life. But a ceremonial mode of religion presents a way to the attainment of divine grace which sets aside, or at least relaxes, the imperative obligations of practical duty. It proposes to secure the favour of God in large measure by mere formal observances.

Second, the inclination to a vicarious service of God

Another, and a not less powerful disposition of human nature, to which sacerdotalism commends itself, is the inclination to a mode of faith which promises relief from individual responsibility. The notion is readily embraced that God may be served by us in some other way than by our personal repentance and righteousness. We find a sense of satisfaction and rest in the belief that the burden of religious obligation may be borne by others on our behalf. And a system of faith which consists mainly in external rites accords with this belief. Because it makes the functions of the ministry all-important, it lessens correspondingly the sphere of the individual conscience. The principle of sacerdotalism is, that whatever needs to be done in the province of religion is to be mainly done by "the Church,"[1] not by the individual. The tenets of "the Church" and the rules of "the Church" are to decide everything; while the same body is regarded as holding a mediatory position in reference to the offering up of divine worship. Thus,

---

[1] That is, by the *clergy*. The misuse of the term church to signify the clergy is made the subject of some observations in Chapter V.

the limits of personal obligation and accountability are reduced to the smallest possible dimensions. The individual Christian does not require to think for himself, or to feel that his acceptance with God depends on his own spiritual condition. He must trust to his religious directors for his belief, and for the intercessory influences which are to secure divine forgiveness and help. It is evident that such a system appeals to human feelings which are of the most powerful character. The desire to be saved from personal anxiety in regard to matters of faith, and to avoid doubts and speculative difficulties, predisposes the devout mind to accept with only too great readiness the offers of a spiritual guide, who promises relief from the task of having to think and inquire. To relinquish freedom of judgment, to end our fears and uncertainties by ceasing to have any convictions of our own, affords a certain kind of mental repose, the very accessibility of which commends it to devout sentiment. The earnest spirit distracted by religious perplexities is tempted to embrace a system, however unsubstantial its claims, which offers such a simple and speedy deliverance from spiritual trials. And, on the other hand, to those who are undisturbed by religious doubts, and whose chief wish is to render the service of God as free from effort and difficulty as possible, the notion that the ministry possess a vicarious character, and that "the Church" relieves us of a responsibility which would otherwise have to be borne by ourselves, presents attractions not less strong.

Third, the tendency to be influenced by the sensuous.

Among the elements of human nature which are appealed to by the sacerdotal type of religion must also be included our tendency to be influenced by material sources of attraction. While art has legitimate functions to fulfil in connection with religion, it may also be employed in an excessive degree. Used as an aid to intelligent devotion, it serves a high and beneficent purpose; but, when allowed to encroach on the province of spiritual worship, and to engross the attention which should be given to truth itself, it becomes a source of evil. There is therefore a danger of material adornment and imposing ceremonies being so profusely and extravagantly employed in Christian worship as to lead to bad results. They may be made so prominent as to overshadow the essential verities of Christianity. The sentiment of admiration for external display, or of reverential regard for what is outwardly solemn, may assume the place of true devotion. Now, the excessive development of such elements of worship is a natural feature of a priestly system. The very nature of the views which it embodies inevitably leads to this result. The notions of mysterious sanctity and power with which it invests the clerical office, and the importance which it assigns to matters of ceremonial, tend to a lavish use of material show and form. And this very fact, while it constitutes a source of evil, is also a powerful means of attraction. A Church which surrounds itself and its services with ritualistic accessories, though it maintains an untrue idea of worship, maintains an idea which commends itself very strongly to a natural tendency of human feeling. It appeals to the imaginative and emotional susceptibilities of our nature. It readily affects those whose minds are open to the influence of external things, while they have not impressions of a deeper kind. Sensuous and ornate elements of worship, such as peculiarly characterize the sacerdotal type of religion, have thus a powerful effect in giving it ascendancy over the mind.

Such are some of the chief causes in human nature, which serve to account for the existence of sacerdotal views, and for the extent to which they have been manifested in the history of Christianity. These views are rather the result of certain strong natural feelings than of any special religious conditions. Their early rise and growth in the Christian Church, their long domination of Christian faith, their reappearance in Protestantism after they had been expressly abjured, and their prevalence even now over so large a part of Christendom, all testify to the affinity which they possess to some of the most powerful human dispositions. The inclination to make the minister of religion a priest, and to hand over to him the transaction of spiritual concerns; and, at the same time, to regard the forms of religious worship as mystic sources of divine influence; is indeed one of the strongest, as it has been one of the most disastrous, of religious tendencies.

II.

Puritanism the opposite extreme.
The object of Puritanism, on the other hand, has been to meet and counteract this tendency. It is the form of opinion most utterly and literally

opposed to Sacerdotalism. We use the term Puritanism in these remarks with a general meaning, as designating a mode of ecclesiastical thought and feeling, which has not been limited to one period alone, but which belongs to the general history of religion.[1] It is the severe and ascetic type of ecclesiastical opinion, as Sacerdotalism is the type which is characterized by the extreme development of ceremony. Each school of thought has exercised a powerful influence on religion. The conflict between them has left many important traces in the past, and both forms of opinion are still active elements of religious thought. We have endeavoured to point out, in the previous part of this chapter, that Sacerdotalism, though it has grown out of Christian truth, and involves

[1] The term "Puritan" was first applied after the Reformation to those who refused to conform to the ceremonies of the Church of England on the ground that the change effected in it from the usages of the Church of Rome had not been sufficiently thorough. The word, however, came to be employed to designate this party on account also of the extremely rigorous principles according to which they sought to regulate everything relating to human conduct, and the austere habits of life which they cultivated. It is in the former signification that we at present make use of the term. Puritanism is referred to in this chapter as representing a tendency relating to ecclesiastical matters and forms.

important facts of Christianity, is, nevertheless, a perversion of the genuine doctrine and spirit of the religion of Christ. The result of our consideration of Puritanism will be to show that, earnest and faithful though its contentions against ceremonialism and priesthood have been, its principles have erred by extravagance on the opposite side. As the Sacerdotal view of religion errs in the one direction by overestimating the ritual and official elements of the Church of Christ, Puritanism errs by excess in the direction of austerity and rigour.

Theory of Puritanism. The Puritan theory may be stated thus:— 'The corruptions of Christianity represented by sacerdotalism are the result of the growth of sensuous elements in connection with worship. When the use of art and external adornment is once permitted in the worship of God, men advance to greater and greater license in this direction. It is therefore necessary, in order to the preservation of the Church of Christ from priestly and ritualistic influences, that there should be a studied and severe abstinence in connection with religion from everything which tends to please the senses. All elements of external attraction therefore, whether as regards the edifice in which worship is offered, or the manner and forms of devotion, ought to be excluded from the service of God. Thus, and thus alone, can the worship of the Christian Church be kept pure. Only in this way is superstition to be avoided.'

This ascetic view of divine worship has its origin in the same sources as serve to explain the existence of religious asceticism generally. In all ages of the history of the Church there have been those who have been disposed to assign extreme prominence to the sterner aspects of piety, who have been less influenced by the love and hope of Christianity than by the demands of the divine law, who have been inclined to contemplate rather the evils of life than its advantages and enjoyments. This fact is due, no doubt, in some measure, to natural temperament. Modes of religious feeling reflect, to a certain extent, the constitutional tendencies with which they are connected. The severe form of Christian earnestness, which would exclude from the sphere of Christianity whatever is joyous and beautiful, is often the result of a disposition of mind which is by nature unjoyous and stern. But there is another

Puritanism a form of the ascetic religious tendency.

cause which operates at times very powerfully in the same direction—a cause lying outside our spiritual nature. When error and evil assume specially alarming proportions, they call forth on the part of those who are zealous for truth opposition so keen and uncompromising, that it is often tinged with a rigour and severity of spirit far beyond what the circumstances of the case really justify. In their enthusiastic detestation of the abuses which they condemn, they assume a position of the most extreme contrariety to them. Thus it has been a common event in the history of Christianity for those who are devout and earnest to proclaim their disapproval of the excesses and follies of social enjoyment by a course of austere self-mortification. The anchorites, whose piety took the form of seclusion in desert places and self-inflicted suffering, were but an example of this mode of religious feeling. The system of monachism rests mainly on the same principle. So do all those cynical and gloomy forms of religious thought and usage, which would make Christian faith essentially antagonistic to social pleasure. The idea which underlies them all is, that, in order to cure the evils which are connected with what is attractive and pleasing in the things of the world, we must go to the opposite extreme from them, and cultivate a spirit of severity. Asceticism, in short, is to be explained to a great extent by the recoil of religious feeling from the evils of what is joyous and attractive in human life; and, while it involves serious error, it is, at the same time, an obviously natural tendency of religion.

Now, the puritan theory of worship is merely, as we have said, a particular instance of this fact —it is the principle of asceticism applied to the forms and circumstances of worship. When, shortly after the Reformation, a feeling of violent hostility to ceremonies became widely developed, and the doctrine came to be extensively maintained that the rites and external accompaniments of devotion must be cut down to the most meagre dimensions, in order to provide an effectual cure of superstition, this was only the principle which the ascetic school had, in one form or another, held in former ages. The Puritan of Reformation times was but the successor to an idea, which had been maintained in every period of the Church's history—the idea that austere rigour in the opposite direction from an evil is the true way to remedy it.

Development of this phase of religious feeling after the Reformation.

It is unnecessary to enlarge on the part which was sustained by the puritan movement after the Reformation, and on the influence which it has exercised on the subsequent history of Protestantism. We have already described the rise and growth of sacerdotal views, which followed the Reformation. The development of puritanism was a natural concomitant of that change. While the one tendency was in the direction of increased ceremonial, the other was in favour of extirpating everything attractive from the services of the Church. While one party had substantially for its object the assimilation of Protestantism to the system of the Church of Rome, the other insisted that the only safety of Protestantism was to be found in making its forms and usages as utterly different as possible from those of that Church. The stern opposition of puritanism to the employment in worship of what is outwardly pleasing was defended as an absolute necessity. Nothing but this, it was argued, could save the Protestant Church from relapsing into the worst errors of the faith of Rome. So long as an attractive ritual was maintained, so long as there was anything to gratify the senses in connection with religious services, the danger of apostatizing from Christian purity was imminent. There must be an absolute exclusion of all such things from religion, if it was to be kept free from corruption. Such were the arguments which were employed by the Puritans when, subsequently to the Reformation, they became a great ecclesiastical power. The principle, as we have seen, was by no means a new one; but was in substance the same as that involved in the ascetic views of religion, which, from the earliest times in the history of Christianity, had existed in various forms. And, while the idea of puritanism thus belongs to times long anterior to those in which the name appears in history, while it is a religious tendency that has been manifested in every age, it continues still to be extensively maintained. The very arguments which were used by this school in the reign of Elizabeth are still familiar arguments. It is still urged by many that the only safety from superstition is an austere opposition to everything of the nature of external attraction in the service of God. The zealous antagonist of Popery often de-

Its present existence.

claims now, as he declaimed then, against the least resemblance to its forms as being the certain forerunner of the direst spiritual corruption. It is still many a time maintained that to depart from a meagre ritual, and to associate divine worship with material beauty or seemliness, is to open the way to the greatest possible evils.

Puritanism objectionable because extreme.

But, though it is unquestionable that these austere ecclesiastical views have had their lofty and noble aspects; not a few of those who have held them having been distinguished by the purity of their purpose, and the vigour and power with which they have striven for great and worthy ends; they are yet liable to the objection which holds against all religious asceticism. Extreme rigour in regard to ecclesiastical observances, like extreme rigour in all other things, is apt to produce the very evils it is designed to prevent. The ascetic principle— the principle that, by the exercise of severe stringency in the opposite direction from an evil, we cure that evil—is not supported by facts. The effect is commonly the very reverse of this. Thus let us take the case of a Church in which the mode of worship is that of the most extreme and studied meagreness. Let us suppose that, animated with the desire of avoiding the dangers of ritualism, it goes as far as may be to the other side,—that it makes its forms as bald as possible; that it refrains from introducing the least element of attractiveness into the appearance of the place in which its services are held; that instruments of music, and painted windows, and all other things that could minister to the gratification of the senses are carefully excluded. Such are the conditions which puritanism accepts as those of uncorrupted devotion. We escape in this way, it is argued, all danger of superstitious practices, for the simple and decisive reason that we are as far away from them as can be. But the argument is utterly fallacious. The truth is that, so far from necessarily escaping superstition in this way, we may only change,— and the probability is that we *do* only change,— one form of it for another. Lord Bacon has truly remarked, "There is a superstition in avoiding superstition, when men think to do best by going farthest from the superstition formerly received."[1] There can be no doubt

It leads to superstition.

[1] Essay on Superstition.

that this observation expresses an accurate estimate of human nature. The fanatical zeal, which leads a man to cultivate puritanic austerity of observance as the one thing needful, is quite as much superstition as the feeling which identifies religion with the extravagances of ritualism. The spirit is the same in both cases. The only difference is in mode. If one man clings with bigoted devotedness to his bald and severe forms, under the belief that they commend him to the divine favour; while another assigns supreme importance to elaborate ceremonial; the distinction between the two is only in manner, not in essential feeling. There is superstition in both instances, opposite as they are in external manifestation.

Similarity between the two extremes. And thus there is, in point of fact, a striking amount of similarity oftentimes between extreme rigour in ecclesiastical matters, and the contrary extreme of sacerdotalism. Milton's well-known sarcasm, " new 'presbyter' is but old 'priest' writ large," has been, times without number, illustrated in the history of the Church. Under an exterior of the utmost plainness of religious usage there frequently exists as bigoted a belief in forms as could be manifested by the most devoted ceremonialist. The stern denouncer of Popish ritual is often as exclusive in his ecclesiastical ideas, and as much wedded to his own religious rites, as the warmest adherent of the Church of Rome could be. It would seem that, when opposition to error is carried to an unreasonable excess, the effect is that human nature arrives at a false state of opinion precisely analogous to that against which its violence is directed. Extravagant severity against an evil ends very commonly in what is much the same as the abuse that is unsparingly condemned. And so puritanism and sacerdotalism have often shown strong points of likeness. The demureness and strictness of the former have frequently been inspired by all the pretension and priestly intolerance of the latter. The religion of the conventicle, with its careful disregard of art, and its contempt of ceremony, has often presented much of the same spirit as the religion of ceremonialism and the cloister.

Such then is the error committed by those who would impose a too strict and austere rule as regards the rites and usages of Christian

The reason of the failure of puritanism.

worship. They deal with the subject too much on narrow, mechanical principles. They overlook the fact that the influence of art may be quite legitimately employed as a means of aiding and expressing the religious spirit; that it is by the excessive use of elements of outward attraction, and not by their use, that harm is done; and that consequently to attempt to keep men in a safe course by means of extreme strictness in this respect is an entire mistake. There is a very curious, and at the same time a most suggestive, illustration given by one of the most prominent Puritan writers of the Elizabethan age, which he intends as a defence of the exercise of rigorous sternness in correcting the superstitious tendencies of our nature; but which really shows very forcibly the absurdity of this mode of dealing with them. He is arguing that, to cure men of their propensity to corruptions of religious worship, it is necessary to go as far as possible to the opposite extreme from these corruptions. This he calls "the cure of contraries by their contraries." And the following is his illustration:—"To bring a stick which is crooked to be straight, we do not only bow it so far until it come to be straight, but we bend it so far until we make it to be as crooked on the other side as it was before on the first side; to this end that, at the last, it may stand straight, and, as it were, in the midway between both the crooks."[1] This, he argues, is the course to be adopted with erring humanity. Its errors are to be corrected by an analogous process to that which is applied to straighten a crooked stick. Its evil propensities must be treated by bending it back to the other extreme; and then, by a kind of reactive force, it will become right in the end. This is an exceedingly apt representation of the remedial agency which the extreme rigorist approves of applying to human nature. He is disposed to deal with the faults and infirmities of men very much in the same way as we might deal with a crooked stick, which we want to make straight.

[1] The book which contains this curious illustration is entitled, "A Replye to an Answere made of M. Doctor Whitgifte againste the Admonition to the Parliament, by T. C." Thomas Cartwright, who is the person designated by the initials, was one of the most noted of the early Puritans; but is now chiefly known on account of the fact that it was against his writings that Hooker directed many of the arguments of his Ecclesiastical Polity.

His method of cure is simply that of utter antagonism to tendencies that may result in evil. His favourite appliances are repression and restriction. It is the essential defect of all ascetic forms of religious thought and feeling that they deal with humanity in this way. They do not recognize those higher and far more powerful springs of action, which consist in living intelligence and unconstrained spiritual life. Puritanism, because it loses sight of these sources of human action, and trusts to the employment of mere rigour, is fundamentally defective. The remedy which it seeks to apply to ecclesiastical abuses is only too correctly illustrated by the comparison of the old divine, to which we have referred. It endeavours to cure one extreme by substituting another. The austerity which it would maintain in the observances of divine worship, if it is a less evil than the excesses of ceremonialism, is still a real evil, and is not infrequently attended, as we have seen, with much of the same spirit.

Teaching of the Scriptures on this subject. While our survey of these two opposite extremes of opinion shows that both of them involve elements of serious error, it is important to observe how the Scriptures deal with those matters in regard to which there has been so much controversy. We must reserve, however, to another chapter the consideration of the general subject of the relation of Scripture to ecclesiastical questions. All that we propose to do now is briefly to indicate the difference between the ground assumed by both of the parties whose views we have described, and the teaching, on the other hand, of Christ and the Apostles.

The entire current of Christ's teaching is diametrically opposed to sacerdotal views and modes of thought. It was one of the chief purposes of His teaching to show that true religion does not consist in external observances. He stood in a position of uncompromising antagonism to Jewish opinion on this subject. He inculcated the practice of the ordinary duties of life as being of infinitely more importance than a regard to religious ceremonies; and He denounced the folly of imagining that God can be pleased with scrupulous attention to matters of ritual.[1] Instead of assigning supreme importance to the office and

Christ's own teaching.

[1] Matt. xxiii. 23-25; Luke xiii. 15; Matt. xii. 7.

functions of the ministers of religion, the whole purpose of the instructions of Christ was to illustrate the supreme value of truth and goodness.

That of the apostolic writings. Nor is the doctrine of the New Testament writings as a whole less strongly opposed than the words of Christ Himself to the sacerdotal tendency. They uniformly declare the need of faith, and prayer, and holiness; but matters relating to rites and forms they always treat as subordinate. They proclaim Christ as the only true Priest and Mediator, and His death on the cross as the only sacrifice for sin.[1] The office of the ministry is described as deriving its sacredness and power, not from mystic spiritual attributes, but from its manifestation of the truth.[2] The Church, so far from being identified with the clergy, is represented as consisting of "all them that love our Lord Jesus Christ in sincerity," and of "all that in every place call upon the name of Jesus Christ."[3]

Sacerdotalism opposed to the nature and spirit of Christianity. The ground of objection to sacerdotalism, which arises from comparing it with the teachings of Christ, and of the New Testament gene-

---

[1] 1 Tim. ii. 5; Heb. vii. 23-24 and 26-28; x. 12.
[2] 1 Cor. iii. 5; 2 Cor. iv. 1-2.   [3] Eph. vi. 24; 1 Cor. i. 2.

rally, is thus not merely its contrariety to certain texts, but its inconsistency with the nature and spirit of Christianity itself. It amounts to a departure from the fundamental characteristics of the religion which Christ and the Apostles taught. The exaltation of the Christian ministry into a priesthood, the elaborate multiplication of ceremonies, and the ascription of mysterious sanctity and saving influence to the external elements of worship, involve an idea of divine service essentially different from that which is represented by the New Testament. Christianity, according to it, is supremely the consecration of the heart and life in the practical duties of human existence. But, on the contrary, the effect of the sacerdotal view of religion is to make it mainly consist in the observance of certain ritual acts. While the view enforced in the Christian Scriptures is, that everything, as regards the attainment of the divine favour, depends on the state of the spirit and life; the principle involved, on the other hand, in a ceremonial system is, that everything is dependent on external conditions. While the announcement of the sacred writers is to the effect that divine grace is accessible directly and equally to all; the idea of sacerdotalism is, on the contrary, that it is concentrated in the hands of the clergy, and can flow to us only through them. While the entire domain of life is described in the New Testament as being embraced within the scope of Christianity, and the holy discharge of daily duty is represented as the true Christian service; the result of the priestly and ritualistic conception of religion is to exalt the ceremonies of the sanctuary above the duties of the world.

<small>The New Testament gives no support to Puritanism.</small> But, although the teaching of the New Testament is thus diametrically opposed to the claims and views of those who would make Christianity a system of priestly power and ceremonial, it gives no support, on the other hand, to the opinion that superstition is to be avoided by the introduction of an austere asceticism into the observances of religion. The views maintained by St. Paul present a remarkable contrast in this respect to the extreme tenets of puritanism. We find him treating questions of religious form with a clear perception of the danger involved in fanatical hostility to rites, not less than of the evils arising from their being held in too great

esteem; and he argues with as much earnestness against the one error as against the other. He saw that, in their headlong zeal in opposition to ceremonies, the party in his day who desired their abolition were losing sight quite as much of the spirituality of true religion as those who too keenly advocated their maintenance. And, therefore, he was careful to point out just what the ecclesiastical rigorist has always overlooked, —that the non-observance of outward forms is not in itself genuine Christianity, any more than the practice of them. According to St. Paul, neither circumcision, nor uncircumcision; neither the keeping of certain days, nor the neglect of them; neither the partaking of certain kinds of food, nor abstinence from them; constitutes true Christian service; but a life consecrated by faith in Christ, and love to Him.[1]

Thus St. Paul discerned, with a wise insight that has often been wanting in the Church since his day, that error finds a footing for itself quite as naturally in the false feeling which makes the *absence* of certain religious forms all-important, as it does in the contrary mistake of regarding their

<small>St. Paul's teaching adverse to the puritan as well as to the sacerdotal view.</small>

[1] Rom. xiv. 2-6; 1 Cor. vii. 18-19; Gal. vi. 15.

presence as of surpassing moment. In his view the spirit of extravagant antipathy to ceremonies is to be deprecated as truly as the feeling of inordinate veneration for them. The position which St. Paul thus assumes is equally opposed to the pretensions of a priestly and ceremonial system of religion, and to the narrowness of excessive rigour.

His principle of Christian liberty.

And the principle which he has laid down as the true principle for the guidance of Christians in reference to the outward matters and observances of the Church is, that they are proper subjects for the exercise of a wise liberty. His counsel to believers in Christ is that, in respect to such things, they should "stand fast in the liberty with which Christ has made them free, and not be entangled in a yoke of bondage."[1] While the rites and external accompaniments of religion constitute a source of most serious evil, if they are elevated to a position of supreme importance; they fulfil certain high and good purposes, when kept in subordination to spiritual truth. Exalted to a place of chief power over our faith, they are essentially bad; employed in

[1] Gal. v. 1.

a secondary relation as expressions of faith, and helps to its exercise, they are full of benefit. Therefore the great rule which St. Paul enunciates with reference to them is, that they should be used in a spirit of freedom. Ceremonies and outward matters are, he teaches, nothing in themselves. They are not Christianity. Christianity is the renewal of heart and life, while forms are but the external appendages of spiritual consecration,—the outward dress which it assumes. And so the true attitude of the Christian in relation to the ceremonial and outward elements pertaining to religious worship is, according to the Apostle's view, earnestly to beware of giving them the chief place in religion; and, at the same time, to employ them in such ways that all things shall be done to edifying. He refrains from inculcating anything on the subject beyond this great general rule. He advocates Christian liberty as regards things outward, with the condition that it is to be used wisely, and so as to promote our own good and the good of others.

CHAPTER III.

THE SCRIPTURES AND ECCLESIASTICAL MATTERS.

"Men have often built up on one or two passages of Scripture an ingenious and consistent scheme, of which the far greater part is a tissue of their own reasonings and conjectures."—ARCHBISHOP WHATELY.

THE SCRIPTURES AND ECCLESIASTICAL MATTERS.

IT was the opinion of the Puritans, and it is still a very common belief, that express Scripture authority must be produced for every ecclesiastical rule and observance. But a fatal ground of objection to this view is that, in point of fact, the New Testament contains no specific commands on these subjects. It does not expressly enjoin on the Christian Church any one mode of government; it does not prescribe a fixed order of worship; and it does not enact the forms and accompaniments with which worship is to be offered. It is true that the supporters of conflicting ecclesiastical systems often appeal to the New Testament in proof of their claims. They argue that the views and practices which

No specific rules in Scripture in regard to ecclesiastical matters.

they maintain are in consonance with what can be gathered from the New Testament as having been recognized in the primitive Church, and that consequently they have divine authority on their side. But, even supposing that their inferences from the Apostolic writings as to the polity of the primitive Church could be relied on —and opinion differs widely as to what its polity really was[1]—the argument is insufficient. For, as we have said, the New Testament does not contain such specific and positive rules on matters connected with Church order as can alone be regarded as constituting express authority.

<small>View of Lord Bacon.</small> The absence from the New Testament of precise commands with reference to ecclesiastical matters leads naturally to the conclusion that it was not the design of Christ or the Apostles to enjoin an exact and unchanging system of polity on the Christian church; but that, on the contrary, it is a subject which is left to be judged of by the discretion of Christians

---

[1] Whately's view seems the correct one that, in point of fact, there is no Church now existing whose institutions and practices are not in some respects different from those of the earliest Churches. Kingdom of Christ, p. 128.

themselves. Lord Bacon expresses this as his opinion—"That there should be but one form of discipline"—that is, government—"in all churches, and that imposed by necessity of a commandment and prescript, out of the Word of God, it is a matter volumes have been compiled of. I, for my part, do confess that, in revolving the Scriptures, I could never find any such thing; but that God had left the like liberty to the church government as He hath done to the civil government, to be varied according to time, place, and accidents, which, nevertheless, His high and divine providence doth order and dispose. For all civil governments are restrained from God under the general grounds of justice and manners; but the policies and forms of them are left free. So likewise, in church matters, the substance of doctrine is immutable, and so are the general rules of government; but for rites and ceremonies, and for the particular hierarchies, policies, and disciplines of churches, they be left at large."[1]

[1] Certain Considerations touching the Better Pacification and Edification of the Church of England. Vol. II. of Works (Ed. 1803), p. 529.

View of the Reformers. This, which is the broad and common-sense view of the ground on which ecclesiastical questions should be judged, accords with the moderate spirit in which the Reformers dealt with matters of church-polity. Luther asserted in energetic terms the liberty of Christians as regards the formal elements of religion.[1] The English Reformers maintained, as we have seen, liberal views of church-government.[2] Calvin, sterner though his system was than that of the English Reformers, did not attribute exclusive value to

---

[1] For a specimen of Luther's freedom of sentiment in regard to forms, see Chapter IV.

[2] "When King Edward died, Cranmer was endeavouring to bring all the Reformed Churches into one communion, each national or provincial Church to retain its own forms and formularies."—Hunt's Religious Thought in England, vol. I., 14. His successors, Archbishop Parker and Archbishop Whitgift, held the same wide ecclesiastical sentiments. Lord Macaulay thus describes the view of the Anglican Reformers in reference to church-government:—"They retained Episcopacy, but they did not declare it to be an institution essential to the welfare of a Christian society, or to the efficacy of the sacraments. Cranmer, indeed, on one important occasion, plainly avowed his conviction that, in the primitive times, there was no distinction between bishops and priests, and that the laying on of hands was altogether superfluous."—History of England, chapter i.

any one mode of ecclesiastical polity.[1] Knox attached more importance to having a mode of church-government practically suited to the exigencies of the age than to the maintenance of a rigid theory. Hence the polity which he adopted was really a combination of Presbytery and Episcopacy, the office of "superintendent" which he introduced into the Scottish Church being so similar to that of "bishop" that it was remarked that the only difference between the two was the difference between bad Latin and

[1] "Neither Calvin nor Luther believed he had discovered the best form of church-government. Guided by right feeling and experience, Calvin was not opposed to a combination of various forms of polity. As he assembled the clergy under his own single presidency to elect pastors, and after preaching to judge of their lives and doctrines, he himself recommended in fact the episcopal element for the larger and more important countries, in order to secure union and order." "He proposed a form of church-government to Sigismund, King of Poland, in which he combined the Episcopal with the Presbyterian elements; his clear understanding perceiving well that a different form of polity was necessary for a great kingdom from that which he had established in Geneva." "Calvin remains the special representative of Presbyterianism, while Luther represents the Consistorial, and Cranmer the Episcopal system, without either the one or the other thinking he had reached perfection."—Henry's Life and Times of Calvin (Stebbing's Translation), vol. i. pp. 400-2.

good Greek.¹ The ritual of the Scottish Church, too, as Knox adjusted it, was a combination of liturgy and unprescribed worship.²

<small>Belief that there must be precise Scripture authority for every ecclesiastical point a Puritan opinion.</small>

But the Puritan movement, which succeeded to the Reformation, was uncompromisingly opposed to the spirit of liberty in regard to ecclesiastical matters. The principle maintained by the party was that of requiring precise Scripture authority for everything. No form of polity, no religious rite, no point of church-order, could, they said, be legitimately admitted, except on the ground of an express rule of Scripture. It was not for man's wisdom to decide what should, or should not, be adopted in the Church. God alone must say, through His Word, what is admissible. That many of those who held this principle were not only thoroughly

---

¹ This is cited by Bishop Hall as the saying of Zanchi, a Protestant divine of Reformation times.—Bishop Hall's Works, vol. x. p. 267.

² See further on this subject what is said in Chapter IV. In this respect Knox and Calvin were at one, as they were also in their readiness to employ a combination of the Episcopal and Presbyterian elements of government; for Calvin also varied the use of his liturgy by occasional extempore prayer.—Henry's Life and Times of Calvin, vol. i. p. 412.

in earnest, but were distinguished by learning and mental power, is evident as well from history as from the Puritan writings. But, at the same time, the evil result which might naturally be expected to arise from the application of such a principle is manifest in the fanciful, and even altogether absurd, interpretations of Scripture with which their arguments abound. Examining the Scriptures with the foregone conclusion that they would find in them rules applying to everything, it inevitably followed that they twisted words and passages, and made them mean what they are not at all intended to teach, and cannot be justifiably accepted as teaching. Thus, in reply to the argument that, as no precise commands in regard to matters of church-polity are given in the New Testament, we may conclude that they are left to be decided by human reason, the following arguments were adduced from Scripture:—That, when Noah made the ark, God gave him express injunctions as to the materials which he was to use, and the size and form of the structure; that, when the tabernacle was about to be erected, God said to Moses: "Look that thou make all things according to the

Its effect on the interpretation of Scripture.

pattern which was shewed thee in the mount;" that, when Solomon built the temple, he had also explicit divine directions to guide him; that, when the second temple was made, God also gave specific commands with reference to its erection; and that, in the vision of God's house described by the prophet Ezekiel, there are most minute precepts as to its shape and proportions and measurements. These statements of Scripture—was the argument—showing that God issued express directions in all these cases, render it certain that He must have appointed a precise and unalterable form of polity for the Christian church![1]

[1] This remarkable line of argument was common with writers of the sixteenth and seventeenth centuries, who felt themselves called on to prove the divine authority of their respective forms of church-government from Scripture. Even Milton adduces this line of reasoning as proof that there must be an express ecclesiastical rule in Scripture.—The Reason of Church-Government urged against Prelacy, Prose Works, vol. I. p. 84. Hooker, on the other hand, justly condemned this line of argument. He says, "As for those marvellous discourses whereby they adventure to argue that God must needs have done the thing which they imagine was to be done, I must confess I have often wondered at their exceeding boldness herein; there being no way in this case to prove the deed of God, saving only by producing that evidence wherein He hath done it."—Ecclesiastical Polity, book iii. 11.

It was on grounds very different from these that the greatest English writer on ecclesiastical polity treated the subject. While Hooker, like Lord Bacon, admits the bearing of Scripture on the general principles of church-order—"touching the manner of governing in general, the precepts that Scripture setteth down are not few, and the examples many, which it proposeth for all church-governors"[1]—he denies that there is an express and complete code of regulations in Scripture with respect to the government and rites of the Church. He maintains that men are left by God to the guidance of their own reason in regard to all points on which a written law is unnecessary; the principles of order which are founded on the wisdom and commonsense of mankind, being not less important in their own place than express revelation.[2] He objects to Scripture being regarded as "the rule to direct us in all things, even so far as to the taking up of a rush or a straw."[3] He argues that to search the Scriptures of God for every matter of form is "to derogate from the reverend authority and dignity

Opinion of Hooker as regards Scripture and ecclesiastical subjects.

---

[1] Ecclesiastical Polity, book iii. 4.
[2] Id., book i. 14.   [3] Id., book ii. 1.

of the Scriptures."[1] Not only so, but those, he says, who are for ever pleading "the Law of the Lord" and "the Word of the Lord" as their authority for every possible point, merely quote, when they are asked to condescend on specific passages, "by-speeches in some historical narration or other, urging them as if they were written in most exact form of law," thus, in point of fact, *adding* to Scripture.[2]

<small>He distinguishes between necessary things and things accessory.</small>
To the objection, that if we thus hold that Scripture leaves many things to the exercise of human discretion we open a way to a dangerous liberty of opinion, Hooker replies that a distinction must be made between what is essential to religion and those elements of religion which are non-essential. Points which relate to matters of church-polity belong, he argues, to the latter class. They are not necessary to salvation, but only "accessory thereunto, so that to alter them is not to alter the way of salvation, any more than a path is changed by altering only the uppermost face thereof, which, be it laid with gravel, or set with grass, or paved with stones, is still the same

---

[1] Ecclesiastical Polity, book i. 15.
[2] Id., book iii. 5.

path."[1] Hooker also points out that to maintain that there must be discipline and government in the Church does not imply that these are to be everywhere the same—"He which affirmeth speech to be necessary amongst all men throughout the world doth not thereby import that all men must necessarily speak one kind of language; even so the necessity of polity and regiment in all Churches may be held without holding any one certain form to be necessary in them all."[2]

The views which Hooker thus expressed on the relation of Scripture to matters of church polity, though stated nearly three centuries since, are greatly in advance of the mode of treatment which has very generally been applied to ecclesiastical questions in more recent times. Champions of each sect and church-system have been accustomed to adduce the Scriptures as sustaining their claims. Whether Bishop or Presbyter, Nonconformist or Churchman, or upholder of any mode of church-government or worship is in the right, can be decided—it has been very commonly held—only by "the law and the testimony." Hence every book of the Bible has been

His views greatly in advance of those held by many in later times.

[1] Ecclesiastical Polity, book iii. 3.   [2] Id., book iii. 2.

ransacked for arguments by contending ecclesiastical writers. Ecclesiastical controversy has been mainly a warfare waged with Scripture texts. To what length this has been carried may be judged of by the use which was made of Scripture when the controversy in favour of the divine right of rival church-systems was at its height. Thus, one of the most erudite supporters of Presbyterianism found in the commandment of God to Moses, when the law was about to be given from Mount Sinai—" Come up unto the Lord, thou and Aaron, Nadab and Abihu, and seventy of the elders of Israel "[1]—evidence of divine authority for the Presbyterian constitution of the Church. Another instance of analogy to the Presbyterian form of polity he discovered in the passage, " Jehoshaphat set of the Levites, and of the priests, and of the chief of the fathers of Israel, for the judgment of the Lord and for controversies." [2] He referred also to these words as indicating the same thing, "Elisha sat in his house and the elders sat with him." [3] The " Moderator " or president of a Presbyterian court he recognized in the text, " Behold, Amariah, the chief priest, is over you

Example of proofs from Scripture in support of Presbyterianism.

[1] Exod. xxiv. 1. [2] 2 Chron. xix. 8. [3] 2 Kings vi. 32.

in all matters of the Lord."[1] Other evidence of the Presbyterian conjunction of pastors and ruling elders in the government of the Church he found in the following passages: "Moses, with the elders of Israel, commanded the people;" "The law shall perish from the priest, and counsel from the ancients;" "Thus saith the Lord, take of the ancients of the people, and of the ancients of the priests."[2] The same divine announced the setting up of a Presbyterian Church in the room of Popery and Prelacy as being foreshadowed by these words in the book of Ezekiel, "If they be ashamed of all that they have done, show them the form of the house, and the fashion thereof, and the goings out thereof, and the comings in thereof, and all the forms thereof, and all the ordinances thereof, and all the laws thereof; and write it in their sight, that they may keep the whole form thereof and all the ordinances thereof, and do them."[3]

[1] 2 Chron. xix. 11.

[2] Deut. xxvii. 1; Ezek. vii. 26; Jer. xix, 1. These citations of Scripture in support of the divine authority of Presbytery are taken from "Aaron's Rod Blossoming, or the Divine Ordinance of Church Government Vindicated," by George Gillespie, Minister of Edinburgh, 1646.

[3] A Sermon preached before the Honourable House of

Episcopacy traced back to Adam.

Nor have such fantastic interpretations of Scripture been confined to one ecclesiastical party. It is evident that, by applying a method of exposition like this, a plentiful array of texts may be adduced without much difficulty to sustain the most opposite opinions. Consequently the supporters of all the various forms of church government have discovered conclusive evidence in Scripture in favour of their respective claims. Thus, while the title of Presbyterianism to divine authority has been urged on grounds which carry us back to the law of Moses, the Episcopal form of polity has had a still more august origin assigned to it. It has been traced back to Adam. The form of government which obtained in the primeval Church was, it has been argued, distinctly opposed to Presbyterian parity. Adam governed the church nine hundred years, and Seth five hundred. The patriarchs were supreme rulers of the Church in their day. Nay, even the Mosaic system, to which Presbyterians have appealed as giving its sanction to their mode of polity, has been pronounced with no less cer-

Commons at their late Solemn Fast, Wednesday, March 27, 1644, by George Gillespie.

tainty to be entirely in favour of an Episcopal form of rule. For was it not characterized by inequality as regards its offices? Were there not distinct orders of priests and distinct orders of Levites?[1]

Such are the absurdities which result from imagining that express Scripture authority must be had for every ecclesiastical view, and for every point of form. Proceeding to interpret Scripture with this preconceived belief, men unconsciously distort it to support their own opinions. They impose on it meanings which it was never intended to convey, and use it to sustain conclusions to which it has no reference whatever. On the other hand, the ground on which Hooker places ecclesiastical questions is incomparably higher, in respect that he claims for them that they should be decided by considerations of reason. Instead of regarding the settlement of them as depending on the critical subtlety which subjects the sacred volume to endless misinterpretation, he defends their being judged by common sense. A right view of the functions of Scripture, as well as of reason, according to him, demands this; for

Rational view of Hooker higher than the Scripturalist view.

[1] Hunt's Religious Thought in England, vol. i. 89.

it is false to imagine that "the light of Scripture once shining in the world, all other light of nature is therewith in such sort drowned, that now we need it not, neither may we longer use it."[1]

The Christian principle with regard to outward matters.

The principle thus vindicated by this writer has a wider range than may appear on a first view. It really involves the fact of the importance and sacredness of rational liberty in religious matters, as opposed to the regulation of everything by stereotyped rule. This is a principle which enters essentially into the teaching of Christ and the New Testament writers. We have already seen that there is a remarkable abstinence on their part from laying down specific commands in reference to matters of ecclesiastical order. And their silence on these points is entirely in accordance with the nature and spirit of Christianity. For it is one of the

[1] Ecclesiastical Polity, book ii. 4. As is well known, vigorous efforts have been made, especially by Keble in his edition of Hooker, to show that this writer may be claimed as a supporter of the High-Church views of episcopacy. But the passages which we have referred to, or have adduced from his work, belong to an entirely different style of thinking, and express sentiments which no believer in the exclusive divine claims of a form of polity could reasonably employ.

chief characteristics of the Christian idea of the religious life that it is not a life formed by external regulations, but consecrated by a sense of divine love, and therefore inspired by a spirit of freedom. The law of Christ is pre-eminently a law of liberty. It does not seek to hem in human conduct by formal restrictions, it does not lay the heart and conscience under minute rules. The influence by which it appeals to men is that of great spiritual principles, and not that of rigid precepts. It gives prominence to what is vital and eternal in religion, and not to those external elements of its existence which are accidental and transitory. Therefore it is that the New Testament does not contain express rules with reference to forms of church-government and modes of worship. Such a code of rules would have been inconsistent with the character of Christianity. As a religion of freedom—of the spirit rather than of the letter—it promulgates all that is of essential and everlasting moment for our guidance, but it leaves the outward shape which faith and devotion may assume, to be moulded by the varying influences of time and human wants. In no other way could Christianity be of universal adaptation to the necessities of the world. Do away with the principle of liberty as regards matters of religious form, and you do away with the possibility of a universal mission for the Christian faith. Were Christianity what the bigoted ecclesiastic would have us believe, exclusively identified with his church-system, it would be nothing more than the religion of an age, or a section of mankind. Its ecclesiastical limitations would prevent its ever becoming more than this. But the large wisdom of the New Testament in not restricting Christians by fixed regulations with reference to church-order and ritual, and so leaving Christianity free to adapt itself in these respects to the many varieties of times and circumstance which must exist in the course of human experience, is in signal contrast to the confined notions of the ecclesiastical partisan.

Difference in this respect between Christianity and Judaism.

In this respect there is a very wide difference between Christianity and Judaism. The latter, as accorded with its merely local and temporary character, consisted chiefly in literal precept. The type of religion represented by the Jewish law, while it had its higher, as well as its more elementary, degree of development, is distinctively preceptive and literal. There are the most explicit enactments with reference to the nature of the ecclesiastical system which the Jews were to maintain. The officials of religion, the place in which worship was to be offered, the manner and order of service, the times of service, and a vast multitude of minute circumstances connected with these subjects, are laid down in express commands, and with copious detail. And the explanation of this wide contrast between Judaism and Christianity is to be found, according to apostolic testimony, not in any real opposition of the two, but in the less perfect character of the former. It was, according to the Apostle, the system appropriate to the time of the Church's childhood, while the latter corresponds to its matureness of spiritual life. Judaism, he affirms, being a mode of education destined for those who were spiritually children, abounded in legal and outward elements; it necessarily brought men under the bondage of things external; it was full of literal enactment. But now, he says, Christ has admitted us into a state of liberty; we are no longer bondservants under a legal system; we are no longer under the elements of the world; Christianity is mainly of the spirit, and not of the letter.[1]

<small>Confusion between Christianity and Judaism a fertile cause of error in regard to ecclesiastical subjects.</small>

Now, the mistake which is made by those who insist on the necessity of an express rule of Scripture being forthcoming for every ecclesiastical matter, and who imagine that human conduct needs to be guided at every point by exact regulations, is that they fail to recognize the difference between Christianity and Judaism. They introduce into the sphere of Christian duty a principle which was appropriate to the character and design of the Jewish system, but which is inconsistent with "the liberty wherewith Christ hath made us free." And it will be observed in reference to those texts and historical allusions of Scripture, which we have mentioned as having supplied proofs of divine authority to contending ecclesiastics, to what an extent they have been taken from the Old Testament. This is only what might have been expected. It arises from the distinctly Judaic nature of the view, which is involved in this idea of church matters. The assertor of the divine right of this or the other

[1] Gal. iv. 1-11.

form of ecclesiastical polity, when he wants to prove his claims by Scripture, is necessarily driven to seek for arguments in the Old Testament; because the ground he assumes is entirely foreign to the New Testament; it is Jewish, not Christian. Hence the ascendancy which has sometimes been attained by the Old Testament Scriptures over the New, in the history of the Christian Church. In the times of the Puritans, and in the days when the Solemn League and Covenant was in the fulness of its vigour, "men's heads," to use the forcible description of Bishop Warburton, "were full of the Jewish dispensation." The very curtains, and candlesticks, and snuffers of the tabernacle furnished material for inference in regard to church matters.[1] Not only the express laws of the Old Testament, but

---

[1] "In the Old Testament there is not an office or an office-bearer but is distinctly determined; in the making of the tabernacle there is not a curtain, nor the colour thereof, not a snuffer, nor a besom, nor an ashpan, but all are particularly set down; yet ye will not get a bishop, nor an archbishop, nor this metropolitan, nor that great cathedral man, no not within all the Bible." This argument against archbishops, bishops, etc., by Mr. Andrew Cant of Aberdeen, in a sermon dated 1638, ends with the ejaculation, "The Lord pity them!"

its historical incidents, its figures, its principles of government, and its most obscure predictions,— all the distinctive characteristics, in short, of its religious faith were introduced into the discussion of forms of Christian polity. It was suggested in the Westminster Assembly of Divines, by one who was evidently not much impressed with this line of argument, that it was desirable that "clear, practical, and express Scriptures, and not far-fetched arguments" should be brought forward; and he added that, though there was much spoken of "the pattern in the mount," he never could find any such pattern in the New Testament.[1] We cannot better understand the

[1] Minutes of the Westminster Assembly of Divines, p. 455. It has been affirmed that the Westminster Confession adopts the principle that express authority of Scripture is necessary in regard to ecclesiastical subjects. The truth is that, as is indicated by the incident above referred to, there were two parties in the Assembly holding opposite views in this matter. While the Presbyterians were abundantly willing to assert and maintain from Scripture the exclusive and divine right of Presbytery, they were prevented from doing so by their opponents, who held opinions of greater latitude. The Confession itself bears traces of this diversity of sentiment: for, while chap. xxi. sec. i. asserts that the only legitimate way of worshipping God is prescribed in the Holy Scripture, chap. i. sec. vi. declares that "there are some cir-

extent to which the Old Testament, and the institutions of Judaism, were appealed to, not by one party only, but by all parties, in support of their respective claims, than from the testimony of the Presbyterian writer, to whose use of Scripture we have already repeatedly referred. This is how he defends himself against the not unreasonable objection that he was not entitled to take the Jewish system as a rule for the Christian Church:—" To me it seemeth strange that both the one side and the other do, when they please, reason from the forms of the Jewish Church, and yet they will not permit us to reason in like manner. The former (the Episcopalians) go about to prove the prelacy by the

cumstances concerning the worship of God and government of the Church, common to human actions and societies, which are to be ordered by the light of nature and Christian prudence, according to the general rules of the Word, which are always to be observed." Dr. Hodge's interpretation of this article is, that "the Scriptures do not descend in practical matters into details, but, laying down general principles, leave men to apply them in the exercise of their natural judgment, in the light of experience, and in adaptation to changing circumstances, as they are guided by the sanctifying influences of the Holy Spirit." (Commentary on Westminster Confession.) This is precisely the position which the supporters of the wider view of ecclesiastical polity have always maintained.

Jewish high-priesthood, and the lawful use of organs in the Church from the like in the temple of Solomon. The latter (the Independents) do argue that a congregation hath right not only to elect ministers, but to ordain them, and lay hands on them, because the people of Israel laid hands on the Levites; that the maintenance of the ministers of the gospel ought to be voluntary, because under the Law God would have the priests and Levites to be sustained by the offerings and altars of the Lord; that the power of excommunication is in the body of the Church, because the Lord laid upon all Israel the duty of removing the unclean, and of putting away leaven out of their houses at the feast of the Passover. Is it right dealing now to forbid *us* to reason from the form of the Jews?"[1]

The Judaic element in religious thought. It may be thought, however, that such illustrations of the erroneous principle of applying Judaic rules to the matters of the Christian Church belong altogether to a past age, and that they have no bearing on existing opinion. But that is very far from being correct. It is no

---

[1] Assertion of the Government of the Church of Scotland, by George Gillespie.

doubt true that a sounder view of the right mode of interpreting Scripture now prevails. The fanciful use of Old Testament texts, and Old Testament incidents, which was regarded as perfectly legitimate in a former age, would not now meet with general approval. Arguments in regard to church-government from the Law of Moses, the furniture of the tabernacle, the ecclesiastical arrangements of the kings of Israel, and the visions of the prophets, would, if they were now urged, be rightly viewed as unworthy of serious attention. It must not be forgotten, however, that a state of opinion often exists where the process of reasoning, of which it would be the logical conclusion, is discarded. The Judaic type of religious thought and feeling has not by any means ceased to subsist as an active influence in the formation of religious notions, though the formal arguments from the Old Testament, by which it used to be supported, are not now in the same repute as formerly. There is still to a considerable extent a tendency of Christian opinion in the direction of what accords rather with the teaching of the Old Testament than with that of the New. It is impossible, for example, to consider the sacerdotal developments of Christianity without observing the closeness of their resemblance to Judaism. The position which they give to the Christian ministry amounts to an assimilation of their office to that of the Jewish priesthood; the very dogma of apostolic succession has its counterpart in the priestly succession of the Jewish Law; while the Christian ritualism of to-day—its profuse use of material symbols, real oblation, the ascription of special sanctity to vestments, the sacrificial altar, and the offering of incense—is little more than a reproduction of the service of the tabernacle and the temple. And, when we regard the Old Testament type of religion from another point of view; when we look at its characteristically legal and stringent nature; it is equally evident that in this respect too it still exercises an important influence on the Christian Church. The rigid ideas of ecclesiastical matters which are often predominant among Christian people are due, it may safely be argued, in no small degree, to the effect of Old Testament modes of thought. Thus the narrow view of ritual, which regards it as unchangeably fixed by divine enactment, is really that which belongs to Judaism, and its express ceremonial laws; but it is quite foreign to the fuller light and life of the religion of Christ. So, too, those exclusive notions of the Christian Church, which identify it with some one external society or mode of government, are Judaic in their spirit: they correspond to the state of things which existed under a system which was local and outward, but they have no affinity to the nature of a communion which embraces without distinction "Greek and Jew, barbarian, Scythian, bond and free." There is also not infrequently the substitution in the Christian Church of the austerity of teaching and discipline, which was characteristic of Judaism, for the freedom of the law of Christ.

It thus appears that the confusion of the principles of the Old Testament with those of the New is a source of error in connection with the interpretation of Scripture, which is not by any means confined to the experience of the past. Modes of belief and of thought which are characteristic of the former are always in danger of being identified with the latter. The Judaizing tend- *Danger of the Judaizing tendency.*

ency which, in St. Paul's day, was produced by the presence of Judaism as an existing system in close contact with Christianity, is a danger resulting not less naturally in later times from the Old and New Testaments being apt to be used without sufficient distinction. Laws and ideas which belong only to the one are liable to be unconsciously transferred to the other. The formal and rigorous spirit of the Jewish Law becomes often the measure of Christianity.[1]

[1] The danger of confusing the teaching which is peculiar to the Old Testament with the principles and truths of the New is a subject which appears to require more attention than is given to it. While the contents of the former are profitable for instruction, and consist in large measure of unchanging truth, it has yet to be remembered that one of the most important features of Christianity is, that it has superseded much that belonged to the former system. There is reason to fear that in the use of the Old Testament this is a good deal overlooked. Persons reading the Old Testament Scriptures, and failing to distinguish between what is permanent in their contents, and what was but temporary, and therefore displaced by Christianity, naturally make great mistakes. Not only did this confusion of the principles of Judaism with those of Christianity make havoc of religious truth in early Christian times; not only does it appear as a source of most serious error in connection with those ecclesiastical controversies of later times to which we have alluded; but it has been a cause of evil in almost every period of the history of the Church. Neander, vol. i. 401; ii. 9; iii. 195, 382; v.

We have seen, then, as the result of our consideration of this topic, that the belief that everything relating to the government and observances of the Church has been prescribed for us in Scripture is not supported by facts. In the first place, it is only by going to Scripture with the preconceived notion that it *must* contain express precepts applicable to matters of ecclesiastical polity, and then making it bear such meanings as would seem to support their own systems, that the advocates of this principle have been able to maintain their argument. And, in the second place, the principle itself,— the principle that everything belonging to the order and forms of the Church is subject to express divine regulation,—involves a confusion of Christianity with Judaism. It ignores the element of liberty which belongs to the former. It puts out of view the fact that an essential characteristic of Christianity is the freedom which it permits in regard to forms; and that, unlike

Survey of previous argument.

3; vii. 111. There can be no doubt that the confusion of Old Testament principles with the spirit and teaching of the New is still a frequent source of religious mistakes.

the religion of the Old Testament, it leaves the Church unrestricted by fixed laws in regard to matters of government and ritual.

Analogy between the divine right of churches and the divine right of kings.

The mistaken ingenuity with which it has so often been sought to prove from Scripture that the divine sanction rests solely on some one mode of church-government resembles the line of reasoning which was common at one time in reference to civil polity. It was maintained by the devoted adherents of monarchy in former days that the person and office of the sovereign are invested with a sacredness derived from the express appointment of God. Texts of Scripture were adduced in abundance to support this claim. Thus it was argued that the command, "Fear the Lord and the king,"[1] shows that the monarch is the representative of the Almighty, and that consequently he reigns by a divine and indefeasible title. It was also asserted that the words, "The sword of the Lord and of Gideon,"[2] are proof that the sovereign possesses direct divine authority. Besides, was not Saul "the Lord's Anointed," and therefore regarded by David as bearing a sacred character?[3] Is it

[1] Prov. xxiv. 21.   [2] Judges vii. 18.   [3] 1 Sam. xxiv. 6.

not a solemn prohibition of the Word of God,
"Touch not mine Anointed"?[1] The fate which
overtook Korah, and Absalom, and Zimri,[2] who
rebelled against constituted authority, was also
quoted as decisive evidence that the office of
the sovereign is invested with inviolable divine
prerogatives. It was with such arguments as
these that a civil monarchy was at one time
defended.[3] Now, however, such proofs from
Scripture in favour of a particular form of civil
government have been discarded as groundless
and absurd: not because the rights of a sovereign are now regarded by those who defend
them as less important or less sacred than
formerly; but because it is now very generally
and very justly believed that they gain nothing
by being supported by such proofs, that, on the
contrary, such an application of Scripture is
entirely mistaken. The true argument,—it is now
acknowledged,—in favour of any mode of civil
government is its inherent excellence; its fitness

---

[1] Psalm cv. 15.
[2] Num. xvi. 32 ; 2 Sam. xviii. 14 ; 1 Kings xvi. 18.
[3] These are some of the arguments used by a Dr. Griffith, in a sermon, which is reviewed by Milton.-Prose Works, vol. iii. 431.

to secure the maintenance of order, and the welfare of those who are subject to its sway.

<small>Ecclesiastical polity to be judged of on general grounds.</small>

The wiser and more moderate notions in regard to civil polity, which thus led men to see that the authority of a government cannot be rested on texts of Scripture, but must depend on its own good qualities, may with equal advantage be applied in the case of ecclesiastical government. The true question in regard to the administration of a church, as of a civil society, really is—Whether its mode of rule is practically wise and efficient? What the particular form of polity by which it is governed may be is not of absolute and essential importance. An ecclesiastical system, which is characterized by enlightened principles, and by effective co-operation in the cause of Christian truth, possesses the strongest possible title to be considered as having the divine sanction, because its fruits are in accordance with the requirements of Christianity. But whether such a system has a gradation of orders of clergy, or only one; whether its constitution is in conformity with the ideas of government maintained by this section of Christian people or the other; whether its ritual accords with this or the other form of religious worship; are not points of vital moment. The conclusion to which the preceding discussion has led us is, that the Christian Scriptures lay down no law whatever in regard to these and similar points. The attempt to make out a case from Scripture in favour of the exclusive divine authority of Bishops or of Presbytery or of any special church system or form of worship, is as idle and unfounded, we believe, as were the arguments from the same source in support of the divine rights of kings. The consideration of expediency—of what is most for the good of men, and will tend most to the promotion of wise and just ends—is the true ground for judging of ecclesiastical, as well as of civil, polity.

It has indeed been strongly objected that to put subjects belonging to ecclesiastical order and form on this ground—to view them as matters in reference to which we are to be guided by a regard to expediency—is to assign to them a position of less sacredness than if we believed them to be fixed by express divine authority. But it may well be answered, first of all, that the question is one of fact; and our investigation of

Mistake of supposing that external divine authority can alone make a thing sacred.

the point goes to show that Scripture really contains no express laws for the regulation of the government and ritual of the Christian Church. Then, as to the assertion that an institution does not stand on the same foundation of sacredness, when its inherent nature is the ground of its claim, as it would if authorized by a direct intimation of the divine will, the truth of this view must be denied. It is a mistake to imagine that evidence of divine authority *ab extra* can alone constitute a thing sacred. Whatever is in itself good and wise, and tends by its own nature to promote truth and goodness, bears the strongest and highest proof of a divine character. It possesses in its internal qualities the most conclusive of all reasons for being regarded as harmonizing with the divine will. And, therefore, instead of its being true that we put ecclesiastical subjects on a lower basis, when we affirm that they should be treated on grounds of reason and expediency, than we would do were we to regard them as requiring a direct command of the Almighty, the result is quite otherwise. We thus really view them in what, according to the teaching of Christianity, is the highest of all lights. For, as we have already remarked, Christianity is opposed by its very nature to the merely legal idea of religion, which seeks to discover a written law for everything, and will not be satisfied unless it can rest everything on outward and verbal authority. It gives prominence, on the other hand, to that inner law of human conduct, which consists in the exercise of enlightened conviction and spiritual wisdom.

And thus it is a mistake to suppose that the dictates of common-sense and reason are a ground of human conduct less accordant with the divine will than positive precepts of Scripture. We give effect to the spirit and the teaching of Christianity only when we assign to the former element the large place which Christianity allows to it. The fallacy of imagining that a literal command or sanction must be had for every point connected with religion is a fertile source of error. Probably there is no more prolific cause of misconception in regard to religious subjects. Fanatical opinion always has its set of texts, on which it builds its superstructure of fanciful beliefs. In the superficial sense of disconnected passages of Scripture, or

Religious errors arise, as a rule, from perversion of Scripture.

in the meaning which a narrow bias attaches to the sacred texts, foundation enough can easily be discovered for the most extreme conclusions. The literalism that demands that every possible subject relating to the Christian faith and the Christian Church shall be explicitly determined by chapter and verse thus leads to serious evils. The effect of it is that persons lay hold on the immediately apparent meaning of certain words of Scripture, while the true intention of the writer is perhaps never sought for. They come to the interpretation of a passage with a certain theory already in their minds, and therefore with a strong disposition to make it sustain that theory at the expense of its real signification. And then the views of Scripture which have been arrived at in this way are apt to acquire a traditional place in religious opinion, which leads to their being received by many with unquestioning belief. Thus it has been to a very large extent, as we have seen, with the use of Scripture in regard to ecclesiastical subjects. When devout fancy becomes the interpreter of the Scriptures, there is no absurdity too great to be deduced from them.

The growth of truer views is now shown in the increasing disbelief of such arguments, which is noticeable in prevailing religious sentiment. The tendency of present opinion is increasingly in the direction of the broad and reasonable idea of Church questions which Bacon and Hooker long ago maintained "That God hath left the like liberty to the church government as He hath done to the civil government, to be varied according to time, place, and accidents, which nevertheless His high and divine providence doth order and dispose," is a doctrine which is necessarily distasteful to the supporters of the divine claims of a special form of church-polity, but it is commended by its moderation and good sense. The particular modes of organization, by which the light and life of Christianity may be diffused, are not of vital consequence except as they are connected with the accomplishment of that result. Men differ, and will continue to differ, as to the external modes which religion should assume. There are circumstances and times to which one form of church-polity is naturally more suited than others. There are special purposes served by one system of ecclesiastical government

Growth of the reasonable view of ecclesiastical subjects.

to which another would be inapplicable. In short, instead of trying to discover in Scripture a rigid rule on the subject, the entire question as to "the particular hierarchies, policies, and disciplines of Churches" is matter for the exercise of a wise discretion, and is only to be rightly decided by keeping in view what is most expedient in each case. High-flown theories in respect to ecclesiastical government are productive of results which are full of evil. In proportion to the magnitude assigned to points of external order is the depreciation of those elements of religion which are of essential moment—justice, charity, and truth. On the other hand, if questions relating to church-polity are treated with a full recognition of the fact that no precise regulations of Scripture exist with reference to them, and that they fall to be determined by those considerations of reason and expediency which guide us in other matters, this is a view which conduces much more to a tolerant and just conception of Christianity.

CHAPTER IV.

CHANGE AS AN ELEMENT IN THE CHRISTIAN CHURCH.

"Because man is changeable, the Church is also changeable—changeable, not in its object, which is for ever one and the same, but in its means for effecting that object; changeable in its details, because the same treatment cannot suit various diseases, various climates, various constitutional peculiarities, various external influences."—DR. ARNOLD.

CHANGE AS AN ELEMENT IN THE CHRISTIAN CHURCH.

It is often maintained that consistent adherence to an ecclesiastical system requires us to cling to all its past usages and rules. To depart, as regards forms of order or worship, from the customs which our forefathers cherished, is to incur, it is thought, the risk of falling into fatal error; while, on the other hand, by steadfastly retaining the practices of former days, by "walking the old paths," we avoid the dangers which beset the introduction of what is new. Let all things remain as they are, and have been, is the counsel of those who deprecate change; for, if alterations are once permitted in the forms of religion, it is impossible to say where these may end.

Opposition to changes of religious usage.

Sometimes unreasonable.

But, good as his intentions may be, the uncompromising opponent of change overlooks an important fact of human experience. Opinion and feeling are ever undergoing alteration. Though it is impossible to assign, in many instances, any explanation of the variations which occur in these respects, there can be no doubt of their continual occurrence. Habits of thought which are congenial to one period are often out of accord with the tendencies of the following age. What suits so well the spirit of one time as to express truthfully its deepest convictions, is often so alien from the character of another that it loses all its original significance. Institutions and observances which, in their own day, did great good, are often so inappropriate to the circumstances of a later age as to be the reverse of beneficial. Now, it is extremely unreasonable to attempt to ignore—as the defender of unvarying uniformity in religious matters does—the existence of this influence. It has its effects as regards Christian faith and life, no less than with respect to other things. While the essence of Christianity remains ever the same, the modes in which it is expressed, and the rites with which it is associated naturally vary with the altered conditions that lapse of time brings with it. And therefore, instead of contending obstinately against all changes, it is rather the part of a Christian society to adopt whatever alteration may tend to good.

For, if a Church stands persistently aloof from the elements of change which are exercising their influence on the sentiments and feelings of men; if it clings with inexorable tenacity to its past traditions, overlooking the new circumstances that are emerging from age to age, the result must be that it will cease to retain its hold on the intelligence and earnestness of the time. The active thought and energy of the world cannot be expected to find anything congenial in an ecclesiastical system that expressly denies the propriety of consulting the claims of the present. The mission of the Church of Christ is concerned pre-eminently with the wants and circumstances of the day. And when, instead of seeking to embrace these, and to bring them within its influence, it holds itself apart from them, and endeavours to keep every-

Evil arising from a church ignoring the necessity of change.

thing precisely as it was in past times, its work must be correspondingly impaired.

Danger arising to a church itself from this cause.

And, on the other hand, isolation from the sentiments and tendencies of the present must produce a most unfavourable effect on the condition and spirit of the Church itself. For, when the influence of the fresh mental activity of the age is allowed to exercise its proper power in the sphere of religion, it has a salutary result. Contact with the ever-changing conditions of thought and feeling is essential to the health of religion. It is when overgrown with traditional prejudices that sacred institutions become corrupt and dangerous. It is when faith and devotion stand most aloof from the life and stir of the intellectual and social world that they are most apt to degenerate into superstition. The influence of the life of the day is, with all its drawbacks, a beneficial influence. If we look back on the history of the Church and observe the nature of the corruptions from which it has most deeply suffered, we see that these corruptions have been the result of mental stagnation more than any other cause. The healthful element of change excluded from the province of religious things, it becomes fertile in all those evils which spring from spiritual changelessness. The prevalence of blind credulity, the ascription of a mystic influence to the material elements and actions of worship, the power of the priesthood—these great evils of the Christian Church have always been associated with traditionalism. They could not have existed where free play was given to the fresh thought and fresh life of mental progress. It is in the spirit of extravagant veneration for the past that they find their support. A religious society which claims to occupy so sacred a position as to be above the necessity of change is a congenial home for false forms of faith and piety.

Now, the view that unvarying uniformity should characterize the Church of Christ was not by any means the opinion maintained by the Founders of Protestantism. They were very far from supposing—as many now suppose—that, by keeping the ordinances and rites of religion the same in all times, we preserve it from corruption. On the contrary, they fully recognized the necessity of varying the external modes of religion. They wisely apprehended that the vitality of Christian

The Reformers averse to unvarying uniformity.

devotion must depend, in no small degree, on its not being fixed down to a single outward type; but being allowed to find new forms for itself, as circumstances arise to require them. Thus, when Luther drew up his Order of Divine Service, he was most careful to point out that it was not to be regarded as an unchangeable formulary of worship. "Above all things," he says, "I most affectionately, and for God's sake, beseech all who see or desire to observe this, our Order of Divine Service, on no account to make it a compulsory law, or to ensnare or captivate the conscience of any thereby; but to use it, agreeably to Christian liberty and their good pleasure, where, when, and as long as circumstances favour and demand it." The general remarks which Luther makes on forms of worship are well worthy of attention. "This and every other Order of Divine Service," he says, "is so to be used that, an abuse arising therefrom, it shall immediately be abolished, and another made; just as the brazen serpent, which God Himself had commanded to be made, was broken in pieces and destroyed by King Hezekiah, because the children of Israel were misusing it. For ordinances are intended to serve for the furtherance of faith and love, and not for the detriment of faith. When they no longer perform that for which they are designed, they are dead and gone already, and are no more of any value; as, when new shoes become old or pinch, they are not worn any more, but are cast away, and others are purchased. Order is an outside thing. Be it as good as it may, it is liable to be abused. In such case, however, it is no longer order, but disorder. Therefore, no ordinance can stand or is binding of itself; but the life, dignity, strength, and virtue of any ordinance is the just use which is made of it, otherwise it is of no account at all."[1]

The judgment thus expressed by Luther rests on grounds which commend themselves to reason and common experience. It is undeniable that observances, good and useful at first, become in time unsuitable. And it is not less certain that, for religious faith to adhere to external forms and things after they have lost their fitness, is inconsistent with intelligent devotion. It might as justly be insisted, to employ the homely figure of the Reformer, that we should continue to use

Religious forms become effete.

---

[1] Hagenbach's History of the Reformation, vol. ii. pp. 9-14 (Clark's Translation).

articles of dress after they are worn out, as that we should employ religious forms after they have become effete. Every time has its own prevailing mental tendencies; and to give them room for exercise in the Church seemed to Luther essential to the true idea of divine service, and not blindly to adhere to the past.

<small>Early Protestant Confessions on this subject.</small> And the view of the Reformers generally, and of those who set forth the earliest declarations of the Protestant faith, was the same. They were against the doctrine that there must be an unbroken uniformity as regards the outward usages of religion. While the Articles of the Church of England assert the authority of the Church, and the need of preserving ecclesiastical order, they also declare—" It is not necessary that traditions and ceremonies be in all places one and utterly like; for at all times they have been divers, and may be changed according to the diversities of countries, times, and men's manners, so that nothing be ordained against God's Word."[1] We find substantially the same declaration in other early Protestant Confessions. "We at this day," says one of them, "having divers rites in the celebra-

---

[1] Article xxxiv.

tion of the Lord's Supper, and in certain other things, in our Churches, yet do not disagree in doctrine and faith: for the Churches have always used liberty in such rites, as being things indifferent."[1] "Although," says another, "our pastors do not keep the same rites and usages as all Churches; and it is neither possible nor necessary that everywhere in all Churches the same rites and ceremonies should be kept; yet they do not oppose themselves to any good and pious rite. To this effect do they teach, that human traditions ought not to be taken for unchangeable and eternal laws."[2] But perhaps the most striking testimony of this kind which is afforded by the early Protestant Confessions, is that contained in the views of Knox on the subject. We refer to his testimony as striking, because the genius of the system whose foundations he laid is very generally supposed to be so rigid as to forbid any departure from an unchanging, standard; and because the name of Knox is often invoked as if it were synonymous with a severe and inflexible puritanism in ecclesiastical matters. The truth is that Scot-

Knox.

[1] The Second Helvetic Confession.
[2] The Bohemian Confession, 1535.

tish Presbyterianism became infected with that spirit subsequently to Knox's time. In its original form, and so far as it reflected the mind of the Reformer, the polity of the Scottish Church rested on principles which were the reverse of narrow. He fully entertained the anticipation that it would be modified to suit the varying requirements of different ages and places; and not that it would be stereotyped for all time coming. "In the kirk (as in the house of God)," says the Scotch Confession of Faith, drawn up by Knox, "it becomes all things to be done decently and in order. Not that we think that one policy and one order in ceremonies can be appointed for all ages, times, and places; for, as ceremonies (such as men have devised) are but temporal, so may and ought they to be changed, when they rather foster superstition than that they edify the kirk using the same."[1]

Knox's distinction of things necessary and things profitable.

Knox states the same view more in detail elsewhere. He lays down the principle that the worship and order of the Church consist of two elements—things essential and things non-essential.

---

[1] The Confession of the Faith and Doctrine belevit and professit be the Protestantis of Scotland, 1560.

The former element, he states, is inseparable from the existence of the Church, and therefore must be maintained universally and always; the latter, on the other hand, is not to be fixed, but should be variously arranged as circumstances may require. The following are his words:—" There be two sorts of Church policy; the one utterly *necessary*, as that the word be truly preached, the sacraments rightly ministered, common prayer publicly made, that the children and rude persons be instructed in the chief points of religion, and that offences be corrected and punished; these things, we say, be so necessary that, without the same, there is no face of a visible kirk. The other is *profitable*, but not of mere (that is absolute) necessity, as that psalms should be sung, that certain places of the Scripture should be read when there is no sermon, that this day or that day, few or many in the week, the church should assemble; of these, and such others, we cannot see how a certain order can be established."[1] So far was the Reformer from believing that absolute uniformity in such non-essential matters was necessary, that he approved of giving liberty in such

[1] The First Book of Discipline.

matters "to every particular church by their own consent to appoint their own polity."[1] And one illustration which he affords of his opposition to anything of the nature of an invariable rule in reference to the mere externalities of religion is worthy of special notice. The ordinary form of the Scottish service in his day was liturgical, and common prayers were read daily in the chief towns of Scotland. Knox was of opinion, however, that the continual and exclusive employment of an imperative formulary of worship would be apt to lead the people to believe that they could pray to God in no other way. He therefore encouraged occasional deviations from this practice. While the Book of Common Order was the authorized form of prayer, he judged it expedient that sometimes public worship should be offered without it. "In great towns we think expedient that every day there be either sermon, or else common prayers, with some exercise of reading the Scriptures. What day the public sermon is, we can neither require or greatly approve that the common prayer be publicly used; lest that we shall either foster the people in superstition, who come to the

[1] The First Book of Discipline.

prayers as they come to the mass; or else give them occasion to think that those be no prayers which are made before and after sermon." [1] What the Reformer desired was obviously to prevent the popular mind from blindly clinging to a form of devotion. He therefore favoured a measure of variety as regards divine services. He was so far from being of the opinion of those who imagine that unvarying uniformity is the true means of avoiding religious errors, that he apprehended serious danger from constant sameness of observance. His judgment in this respect is the same as that expressed by another Reformer, who says, "Sometimes it is profitable that there should be difference of rites, lest men should think that religion is tied to outward ceremonies." [2]

It thus appears that the original position of the Reformed Churches as regards the subject of changes of usage and ritual is very different from what is often supposed. Many persons seem to think that, when the Protestant faith and worship were settled, everything relating to the forms of religion was fixed for all future time; and they consequently regard the introduction of change

Real position of Reformed Churches in relation to the subject of changes

[1] The First Book of Discipline.   [2] Calvin.

as an essential departure from ancient Protestant principles. But that is not at all the true state of the case. So far from absolutely excluding what is new from the Christian Church, it is a fundamental article of Protestantism that the differences which arise with new times and new circumstances are to be provided for. The testimonies of the Reformers themselves, such as we have quoted, distinctly show that this was their view. It is characteristic of the Church of Rome that she professes to be unchanging and unchangeable. One of the opinions which she condemned as erroneous at the last Œcumenical Council was that "the Roman Pontiff can and should reconcile and accommodate himself to progress, liberalism, and modern civilization."[1] Now, that is a position which, however much it may be objected to in itself, the Church of Rome is not inconsistent in maintaining. Because she claims infallibility, it necessarily follows that she claims also to be immutable. And, moreover, in a priestly system of religion, all traditional usages, and all the

[1] Acts and Decrees of the Most Holy and Œcumenical Vatican Council opened on the 8th day of December, 1869, by Pope Pius IX.

elements of ritual are invested with such transcendent notions of sacredness, that to disturb what the sanction of antiquity has rendered venerable would be to undermine the foundations on which the system rests. But when, on the other hand, the Protestant assumes the same position of antagonism to the influences of the day, he occupies ground which is thoroughly out of accordance with his creed. For the view which he claims to represent is, that faith and worship are not subject to the dictation of an infallible human authority, and do not depend for their value on any human priesthood; but that they are matters of individual conviction and experience—matters in regard to which the living intelligence and the living earnestness of the present are to be freely exercised. It is manifestly irreconcilable with this view to suppose that the Church of Christ should endeavour to ignore those elements of change which are ever operating on the thoughts and feelings of mankind.

It is no doubt true that the feeling of reverent regard for the past is an important influence as respects religious matters. That feeling cannot be discarded without the sacrifice of some of the

Veneration for antiquity apt to err by being indiscriminate.

most elevating associations of Christian belief and worship. The value which is given to forms of religion by their having been in use for ages, and the solemnity with which they are invested by the knowledge that they have expressed the piety of former generations of Christians, constitutes a source of powerful interest. The care, therefore, of a Church should be to maintain this sentiment : to keep entire, so far as may be, those bonds of connection, which unite the present to whatever is best and truest in former times. But, on the other hand, it is a mistake to think that, in order to conserve the precious traditions of the wisdom and piety of past days, it is needful to avoid any departure from the usages which they have handed down to us. An undistinguishing veneration for antiquity prevents our receiving from it as we ought the lessons which it is fitted to teach us. For, in the first place, it has its evil traditions as well as its good : the inheritance which we have derived from it consists not less of errors which stand in need of exposure and correction than of what is true and precious. And, therefore, to adhere without discrimination to whatever belongs to the past is in reality to lose the true benefit of its teachings. It is an unfailing law in the history of social institutions that when they keep rigidly within the attainments of bygone times they decay. There must be endeavour, not only to *retain* what has been reached, but to *advance* on it; otherwise the ground already gained is gradually lost. So that the true conservators of the good and truth of former days are those who, instead of holding blindly by whatever is old, seek the removal from it of deficiencies and evils.

And there is also another fact which is overlooked by those who are such unqualified admirers of the past that they stand out against any deviation from its religious usages. They forget that when transmitted from one age to another, a mode of thought or practice frequently assumes a quite different relation from what it had. Very often—as has been already stated—an institution, or an observance, which, in the circumstances of the time that gave it birth, represented some important truth, survives its meaning, and becomes an abuse. The history of the Christian Church supplies many such instances. Thus, the practice of religious seclusion, when it

Traditional usages cease to mean what they did at first.

first became prevalent among Christians, was the result, to a large extent, of the conditions of the age. To be able to worship God in security, it was necessary in very many cases for the Christians of early times to take refuge in solitary places from the violence of the persecutor. But the custom, which thus arose at first out of the spiritual necessities of the Church, and was expressive of a pure and ardent piety, became a very different thing when continued after the need for seclusion had ceased. The superstitious notions which came to be associated with monastic life were the corruption of what had been at first a true manifestation of religious feeling. And, to take another instance, there can be no doubt that the elaborate symbolism which in early ages was gradually developed in connection with Christian worship, expressed at first certain great religious truths. Men recognized originally in the various ceremonies which were introduced into the Church the representation of spiritual realities. They were to them only the material embodiment of the facts and emotions of an earnest faith. But, in course of time, the truths to which these external observances pointed were for the most part forgotten; and the devotional services with which they were associated became little more than an affair of empty form and lifeless ritual. And yet another illustration may, we think, be found of religious usages losing their true meaning and becoming unreasonable, in those stern puritan notions of religious worship, which grew out of the circumstances of a past age. They were, to a certain extent, a reaction from the violent excesses of the opposite extreme of ceremonialism. They were, on this account, identified with resistance to ecclesiastical tyranny; and therefore their history contains much that is worthy of admiration. But when it is urged that the austere rites and observances of the puritanism of former times are to furnish a law for the regulation of the Church of to-day, and of all coming times, this is to overlook the fact that what arose naturally out of the condition of another period is no longer applicable to the present age. The state of things is so greatly altered, that to cling now with obstinacy to the meagreness of form that was at one time so extensively characteristic of Christian worship, is incongruous and unreasonable.

Religious life cannot be limited to the forms of the past.

Thus the retention of the religious usages of the past is not necessarily a good thing. It may result, and often results, in disadvantage to the life and purity of religion. It is as little in accordance with reason to require that Christians should always continue to employ the same modes of manifesting their belief and devotion, as it would be to insist that men should always utter their thoughts in the same words and phrases as their forefathers, or that the common affairs of life should be carried on according to the customs of bygone times. The obvious answer to the form of social idealism which maintains that mankind would be better if all things could be kept as they were long ago, is, that, even were the notion one that could be realized, it would have no such results as are fancied.. The new things, and the new influences, which are ever coming into existence in the social life of the world, while they may introduce elements of evil, are nevertheless essential conditions of prosperity and progress. The world, were it to remain in a state of unchanging uniformity, would be destitute of healthy life. Now the same thing holds in regard to men *religiously*. It is impossible that

Christianity can possess vigorous life, or can exercise its rightful influence, if it is bound up in the forms of the past entirely. The maintenance of power and vitality in a Church depends largely on its being open to receive the impulse of those varying sentiments and tastes, which are the result of change of times.

Nor can it be justly objected that matters relating to the Church of Christ come under a different rule in this respect from other institutions and things. That is the ground assumed by the ecclesiastical school, which refuses to admit the lawfulness of altering anything in the Church from what existed in the past. It is argued that, necessary and legitimate as it may be to accommodate the usages of ordinary human life to the changing circumstances of the world, ecclesiastical affairs belong to the sphere of divine things, and must, therefore, not be treated on the same principles of human wisdom and policy as are applicable to mundane concerns. But those who take this line of objection overlook an important distinction. The Reformers, as we have seen, were careful to discriminate between things essential and things non-essential in the Church,

Objection that sacredness of religious things forbids change.

and it was to the latter only that they attributed the character of variableness. The *essence and spirit* of Christianity are unchangeable; but it is surely a very false judgment which assigns immutable obligation to the merely external and formal elements, with which its existence is associated. There is surely the widest possible difference between what Luther calls the "outside things" of religion, and its life; between things "necessary" and things merely "profitable," to adopt the distinction of Knox; between that which is "necessary," and that which is "accessory," to employ Hooker's language; between the "letter," and the "spirit," to take the terms used by a higher authority.[1] It is from failing to distinguish between these two very different classes of religious subjects that some of the worst errors of Christian opinion have arisen; and when men stand by old ecclesiastical customs, and old ecclesiastical forms, and maintain that they are to be retained as inviolably sacred, though they belong to another age, and have no longer the same suitableness to the wants of the Christian Church as they had at first; this is but an in-

[1] 2 Cor. iii. 6.

stance of the confusion to which we refer. It is viewing mere "outside things" as if they were vital principles of Christianity. It is as much as to say that Christianity is fixed and confined to these external modes—that it cannot exist except in connection with them. And thus it amounts to putting the *form* above the *spirit* of Christianity.

On the other hand, the introduction of such variation of usage and ritual into the Christian Church as "diversities of times and men's manners" render expedient, represents the all-important principle of Christian liberty in things indifferent. It amounts to an assertion of the superiority of religion to traditional observances. It is a protest against the narrow formalism that would tie Christians down to a single type of religious service. Hence the value which it had in the eyes of the Reformers. When Luther besought men, for God's sake, to throw aside his Service Book, and have another made, whenever there should arise any danger of its becoming an object of superstitious regard, he but expressed the great truth of spiritual freedom. Christianity is not to be exclusively identified with this or the other external rite or custom. Love to Christ, *(marginal note: Importance of Christian liberty as respects outward things.)*

and Christian life and earnestness, naturally clothe themselves in many different outward forms of service. And they must be allowed a large measure of diversity if they are to find living expression for themselves. The sentiments of the Reformers in this respect only represent one of the great characteristics of the religion of the New Testament. As we have already seen, the teaching of Christ and the Apostles is in favour of liberty as regards outward matters. Nothing is more apparent in the New Testament than the subordinate position assigned to rites and the external accompaniments of faith. "The liberty with which Christ has made us free" consists largely, according to St. Paul, in His having brought us into a state of exemption from the yoke of a rigid system of forms,—in His securing for His people emancipation from the bondage of a compulsory law of ceremonies. It is the part of Christians to *use* outward observances and matters of order, so far as they are serviceable to the promotion of the Christian life; but it is their right and duty not to be slavishly *subject* to them. They are but means to an end, and, therefore, are never to be employed but with a wise freedom.

It is true, no doubt, that the exercise of this freedom is by no means unattended with danger. To deviate from common usages, especially if these have the sanction of long-continued observance on their side, is a course serious enough to deserve the most careful consideration. At the same time, it is really no good reason against the introduction of what is new, that it sometimes leads to evil consequences. When it is argued that, by departing from the existing practices and forms of a church, we may open the door to other and mischievous changes, that is an objection which might be made to all improvements whatsoever. There could be no such thing as amendment of the conditions of human existence were men to act on this principle. Not only so, but it should also be remembered that to introduce salutary and timely changes is the only means of avoiding those which are disastrous. The worst contingencies which happen in institutions and communities are those which come because of wise changes not having been made in time. The longer needful improvements are resisted, the more perilous is the spirit of innovation when once it sets in. Extravagant severity of ecclesiastical

Danger attendant on change not the only danger to be considered.

discipline, for example, in one age, is followed by irreligion in the next. The excesses of ritualistic zeal have often been nothing more than the violent reaction from fanatical repression of ceremonies. An attempt to control by rigorous measures the current of opinion has frequently no other result than to produce a plentiful crop of heresies. Thus the extremeness with which men oppose themselves to change leads to the very consequences which they seek to avoid. They think to keep everything safe by maintaining a policy of unyielding resistance to the new influences amidst which they are placed; and at last the tide of feeling, which might have been usefully directed by timely wisdom, but which has been stubbornly opposed, becomes a violent and dangerous power.

So that, although the introduction of changes into the forms of religion is admittedly capable of abuse, it is in this respect only like other things which have their useful purpose. The possible evils which attend it are not to be prevented by unqualified opposition to it. This is as absurd as it would be to maintain that "because children may perhaps hurt themselves with knives, therefore the use of knives is to be taken quite and clean from men also."[1] While, therefore, it is needful to guard against an unregulated and inconsiderate fondness for novelty,—and even the excessive dread of change, which is felt by many, is not wholly without its use as a counteractive to this tendency,—there can be no doubt, on the other hand, that it is a shortsighted judgment which overlooks the possibility of evil consequences from the opposite extreme.

One of the most curious and instructive comments on the opinion of those who urge the necessity of adhering to the religious usages of the past is supplied by a comparison of one past age with another. The result is to show that the same fluctuation of religious observances occurred in former times, as is still occurring. The advocate of unchanging uniformity, when he appeals to what is old as if it had always been the same, forgets this. He forgets that the history of bygone days presents as great variations of religious form as does the present age in relation to those preceding. Take for example the Presbyterianism which claims descent from

History of the past as bearing on this subject.

---

[1] Hooker's Ecclesiastical Polity, book iv. 12

the Scottish Reformation. Its past history exhibits wide differences in regard to order and ritual. If, for instance, we go back to the age of Knox, we find that the system then embraced, as has been noticed, a liturgy, and daily public prayer. The Presbyterian service of that age, while it was of a severer style than characterized that of the Church of England, was possessed of much external seemliness and respect for form. But, descending to a subsequent period in the history of Scottish Presbyterianism, we find a widely different condition of things. With the growth of the Puritan spirit there arose opposition to liturgical forms, and a disregard of ceremony in worship, which led to the meagreness that came to be identified with Presbyterian services. To give no place to the indulgence of a cultivated taste in regard to the external circumstances of devotion, to banish from the sanctuary everything of the nature of ornament, to exclude musical culture from divine praise, and, in short, to divest religion of all outward attractiveness, was considered an essential ecclesiastical duty. Nor can it be said that there has been a continuous sameness of Presbyterian usages in later times. Each age has brought its changes. Thus, if we revert to the period represented by the Westminster Assembly of Divines, we find that the nature of the services which belonged to that time was such as at the present day would be intolerable. A prayer was often two hours or more in length. A service was frequently continued without intermission during an entire day. The following is an account of a service held during the sittings of the Westminster Assembly:—"We spent from nine to five very graciously. After Dr. Twiss had begun with a brief prayer, Mr. Marshall prayed large two hours most divinely, confessing the sins of the members of the Assembly in a wonderful, pathetic, and prudent way. Afterwards Mr. Arrowsmith preached an hour; then a psalm; thereafter Mr. Vines prayed near two hours, and Mr. Palmer preached an hour, and Mr. Seaman prayed near two hours. After Mr. Henderson had brought us to a sweet conference of faults to be remedied, Dr. Twiss closed with a short prayer and blessing."[1] That this extraordinary prolixity was not exceptional, and

[1] Principal Bailie's Letters and Journals; Letter 59.

did not arise from the particular conditions with which this service was conducted, is shown by what we are told of one of the most eminent preachers of the time. "On the public fasts, which in those days returned pretty frequently, his common way was to begin about nine in the morning with a prayer for about a quarter of an hour, in which he begged a blessing on the work of the day. He afterwards read and expounded a chapter, or psalm, in which he spent about three quarters; then prayed for about an hour, preached for another hour, and prayed for about half an hour. After this he retired and took some refreshment for about a quarter of an hour or more, the people singing all the while, and then came again into the pulpit, and prayed for another hour, and gave them another sermon of about an hour's length; and so concluded the service of the day at about four o'clock in the evening, with about half an hour or more in prayer."[1]

Such religious services suited, no doubt, the nature and tendencies of the day. They accorded somehow with the phase of devout and

---

[1] Life of Mr. John Howe, by Edmund Calamy, D.D.

earnest feeling which was characteristic of a period of deep, but austere, piety.[1] One has only to

[1] While it is safe to admit that this style of service would not have been customary at a former period had it not been in conformity with the religious feeling of the time, it does not follow that it was in itself consistent with the highest idea of devotion. South, who tells us that the Puritans sometimes carried on their services from seven in the morning till seven in the evening, and that "two whole hours for one prayer used to be reckoned but a moderate dose," denounced, with the vigorous language and pungent wit of which he was so great a master, the folly of their mode of worship. One of his illustrations in favour of short prayers, rather than long, is worthy of quotation :—" That subject pays his prince a much nobler and more acceptable tribute who tenders him a purse of gold than he who brings him a whole cart-load of farthings." (Sermon against Long Extemporary Prayers.) On the other hand, Cotton Mather, in his very curious account of New England Puritanism, dilates with admiration on this feature of the services ; and, at the same time, he shows, by the way he refers to the long prayers which were customary, that they were really effusions partaking quite as much of the nature of sermons as of that of prayers, and that they were listened to by the congregation as such. He says of one of the New England pastors that "it transported the souls of his hearers to accompany him in his devotions, wherein his graces would make wonderful sallies into the vast field of the entertainments and acknowledgements with which we are furnished in the new covenant." Again he says, "New England can show even young ministers who, for much more than an hour together, pour out their souls unto the Almighty God in such a fervent copious, and yet proper manner, that *their*

imagine, however, the introduction of such a style of worship into modern times, in order to see the absurdity of the argument that there should be an unvarying uniformity of ecclesiastical usage.

<small>Conclusion.</small> And now, to sum up the considerations which we have adduced on the subject of change in religious forms, it appears, to begin with, an entire mistake to suppose that unvarying sameness was originally designed to be a characteristic of the order and worship of Protestant Churches. That view is in direct contradiction to the view of the Reformers themselves. It has arisen from the natural but mistaken belief that, to prevent all deviation of religious observances from those of former times is the right way to save religion from error. The Reformers, from the very position which they occupied as opponents of the traditional faith and ceremonies which had involved the human mind in error and superstition, were preserved from this mistake. They

<small>*most critical auditors can complain of nothing disagreeable, but profess themselves extremely edified.*"—Magnalia Christi Americana, or the Ecclesiastical History of New England from 1620 to 1698.</small>

wisely and truly judged that the Christian Church must not, if she is to be living, be bound down by inflexible rules in reference to the details of order and observance. And, while this is the principle which guided those who were leaders of the Reformation, the entire history of Christian faith and worship shows the wisdom of this principle—the wisdom of allowing such freedom in reference to matters of religious form as will enable them to be adapted to the ever-varying conditions of the world. The Christian Church should reflect in her methods the circumstances of the time which she has to serve. A blind adherence to tradition destroys her influence for good. And, moreover, it is to be borne in mind that timely concessions to the new wants and new feelings of an age are the only effectual means of avoiding violent and dangerous revolution. The most mischievous changes are those which are caused by excessive hostility to change.

CHAPTER V.

WORDS AND PHRASES CONNECTED WITH THE CHURCH.

"There is hardly any rank, order, or degree of men, but more or less have been captivated and enslaved by words."—
SOUTH.

WORDS AND PHRASES CONNECTED WITH THE CHURCH.

No one who would form a just opinion in reference to matters relating to the Christian Church can afford to disregard the part which words and phrases have borne in connection with them. It is to this source that not a few of the gravest ecclesiastical errors are in a considerable degree traceable. Many of the modes of expression which have passed into common use in relation to the Church are foreign to Scripture; and some of these, while they are apt to be accepted without question because they have been long familiarly employed, are liable to produce misapprehension. Numerous phrases, again, which belong to Scripture have come to be used ecclesiastically in a different

Importance of words and phrases in connection with ecclesiastical opinion.

sense from that which they possessed at first, and therefore readily lead to confusion and mistake. It is therefore of the greatest importance that we should take into account the influence of terms and phrases in relation to ecclesiastical subjects and should make allowance for the power which they exercise in the formation of opinion.

We do not propose to examine with anything like fulness of detail a subject which is so extensive. All that we intend to do is to refer to some of those more outstanding instances, in which the recognized forms of speech connected with subjects belonging to the Christian Church tend to produce misconception.

Classification of the subject. There are three influences of an important character which may be especially particularized as affecting the use of words and phrases connected with the Church; and we propose to group the illustrations to which we shall refer according to these causes of confusion or error. In the first place, the sacerdotal form of religious thought has exercised a powerful effect in impressing its mode of belief on words; so has also the dogmatic tendency—the tendency in the direction of abstract statements of Christian truth and doctrinal teaching; while a third fact which has led to a misuse of terms relating to the Church is to be found in the liability of phrases to assume a more limited and partial meaning than properly belongs to them.

I.

The influence of the Sacerdotal Tendency on the use of words is forcibly illustrated in the term "Church" itself. There are different phases of meaning which belong to that term as employed in the New Testament. It signifies sometimes Christians universally, viewed as a collective body,[1] and in other instances it refers to individual societies of Christians.[2] Sometimes it designates the Christian communion regarded in its ideal and ultimate character, in which case it is represented as consisting of "saints," "the faithful in Christ Jesus," "the sanctified," and by similar exalted descriptions,[3] and it is applied at other times to the communion of Christians viewed in its actual condition as having in it a mixture of good and evil elements.[4] But whatever may be

The term "Church."

[1] Eph. i. 22; Col. i. 18. [2] 1 Cor. i. 2; Gal. i. 2.
[3] Eph. i. 1; v. 27. [4] Gal i. 1-6; Rev. ii. 1.

the particular reference of the term in any given passage of the New Testament it always includes Christians without external distinction of any kind. Those who constitute the Church, or an individual Christian society, are, according to the New Testament, Christian people. It is in the union and co-operation of its members as a whole that the essential principle of the existence of an ecclesiastical body is represented as consisting, each Christian having certain functions to discharge which are of vital importance to the entire society.[1]

When, however, in the post-apostolic age the sacerdotal view of the Christian ministry came to prevail, the view which exalted them to the position and authority of a priesthood, a change of the most momentous kind was introduced into the use of the word. The Church now began to be regarded as merely synonymous with the clergy. The people were left out of account as members of the communion of Christ. And there can be no doubt that this perversion of a Scriptural and primitive term was much better fitted to serve the ends of those who desired the ascendancy of

[1] Rom. xii. 5; 1 Cor. xii. 12-31.

the clergy than if they had advanced their pretensions openly and undisguisedly, for it had the effect of magnifying the power and prerogatives of the clerical order without clearly appearing to do so.[1]

The same misapplication of the term is still very common, and it is still all the more dangerous that it is not immediately apparent in many of the instances in which it is used. Very frequently, when the "Church" is spoken of in terms of veneration, and its attributes are insisted on with expressions of subserviency and praise, it is really the clergy who are meant. Thus, when divine authority is claimed for the "Church," when the traditions of the "Church" are referred to as constituting a rule for Christians, and when the "Church" is represented as the appointed means of salvation, these assertions are, in point of fact, made—in many cases at least—not of the Church in the New Testament sense of the word at all,

---

[1] "The clergy began to draw to themselves the attributes of the Church and to call the Church by a different name, such as the faithful or the laity, so that to speak of the Church mediating for the people did not sound so shocking, and the doctrine so disguised found ready acceptance."— Dr. Arnold's Sermons on the Christian Life, Introduction.

but of the ministry only.[1] Now this involves a fundamental subversion of the true idea of the

[1] Of course this use of the term is constantly made by the Church of Rome, the clerical element being all-important in that body, while the people occupy a subordinate and subservient position. Coleridge thus refers to the same perversion of the word to designate the clergy as characteristic of the High Church party in the Anglican communion :—" As far as the principle on which Archbishop Laud and his followers acted went to re-actuate the idea of the Church as a co-ordinate and living power by right of Christ's institution and express promise, I go along with them ; but I soon discover that by the Church they meant the clergy, the hierarchy exclusively, and then I fly off from them in a tangent. For it is this very interpretation of the Church that, according to my conviction, constituted the first and fundamental apostacy."—Literary Remains, vol. iii. p. 386. It is a curious circumstance that the Second Book of Discipline, though drawn up by Presbyterians whose hostility to the priestly system of the Church of Rome was intense, accepts as legitimate the very interpretation of the Church which is identified with priestly views :—" The Kirk of God is sumtymes largelie takin for all them that professe the evangill of Jesus Christ, and so it is a company and fellowship not onlie of the godly, but also of hypocrites professing alwayis outwardly ane true religion. Uther times it is takin for the godlie and elect onlie, *and sumtymes for them that exercise spiritual function amongis the congregation of them that professe the truth. The Kirk in this last sense hes a certaine power grantit be God, according to which it uses a proper jurisdiction and government.*" Presbyterianism has sometimes been quite as high church and priestly in its own way as the followers of Laud.

Church of Christ. For unquestionably the view of it which, as we have seen, originally existed, was that it consists of Christians in general. The usurpation of the name by the clerical order alone, such as is common in all ecclesiastical bodies which are infected with sacerdotal views, is therefore an essential departure from New Testament teaching. It ignores the position of the Christian people as members of the Church. Its effect is to represent the clergy as all-important and the Christian people as only the submissive subjects of their authority.[1]

[1] This misapplication of the term Church to signify the clergy lies at the root of the false meaning assigned to the passage, "Thou art Peter, and upon this rock will I build my church."—Matt. xvi. 18. The interpretation attached to this passage that Peter was to be the foundation of an order of clergy who should bear rule over the spiritual concerns of the world, rests on the mistake of overlooking that the church means, in the New Testament, not the clergy but the Christian people, the real sense of the words thus being that *the community of believers* would be founded on Peter's apostleship and ministry, on account of his being the leader in proclaiming the truths of Christianity. So too that other passage which is adduced as a proof that there is an infallible divine order of ministry who are the judges and interpreters of the will of God—"the church of the living God, the pillar and ground of the truth" 1 Tim. iii. 15—is seen at once to mean something quite different when the church is taken in its true sense. Then

"Clergy" and "Laity." But while the misuse of the word Church to signify the clergy is the strongest and most prominent evidence of the effect of the priestly tendency of thought in moulding forms of expression to suit itself, there are also other terms which clearly bear the impress of the same influence. Thus, although the distinction of "Clergy" and "Laity" is one which, if understood in a limited sense, is not only legitimate but so natural and convenient that it forms an appropriate distinction of common language, it admits, at the same time, of being made to convey, and has often been used by the believer in sacerdotal opinions to convey, an utterly false idea. It is taken by him as meaning that there is a difference of an intrinsic and essential character between the two classes. When the importance of the clerical office is so exaggerated as to invest it with elements of supernatural sanctity and power, the result is necessarily to create a vast separation between it and the position of the general body of Christians.

it conveys the fact that *Christian men and women*, as the Church of the living God, constitute the stay of the truth by maintaining and advancing the cause of Christ in the world.

The ministry are thus placed on an essentially different level from the people: they become the sole agents in religious affairs, the function of the people is but to believe and obey. Now, the distinction of "clergy" and "laity" has been very largely employed throughout the history of the Christian Church in this exaggerated and untrue meaning. Instead of marking only that difference between the ministerial office and the standing of the general community of believers, which it is right, and indeed unavoidable, to designate, it has been laid hold of by the priesthood, and made largely to subserve the maintenance of their claims.

The same thing is true of the distinction between the "Sacred" and the "Secular." The employment of these and kindred terms to denote the difference between the ecclesiastical sphere and the sphere of the world, while it rests upon a certain basis of truth, has been productive of serious error. There is, no doubt, a restricted sense in which such forms of expression are not only lawful, but indispensable. Some difference must be made between those services, and seasons, and places, which are appropriated to the special

"Sacred," "Secular," etc.

worship of God, and those which are not. But
nothing, on the other hand, can be clearer than
that the Christian Scriptures deal with religion
as including the entire life, and that the service
of Christ is regarded by them as consisting quite
as truly in the performance of worldly duty as in
acts of express devotion. And consequently any
distinction which is made between the two should
be of a qualified and limited nature. We have
only to glance, however, at the traditional phraseology, which is used to represent this distinction,
in order to see that it receives in ordinary
language a recognition which is exaggerated and
misleading. The rites and services of the sanctuary are referred to in conventional language as
"sacred," "religious," "holy," "divine"; while,
on the other hand, things which belong to the
domain of the world are "secular," "common,"
"worldly," "profane." Now, even admitting that
these terms, from having been long in use, are
employed to a great extent in a merely formal
sense, there is yet a false notion lying at the root
of them, and they help to encourage an untrue
estimate of the comparative importance of ecclesiastical observances and daily duty. The existence

in ordinary language of these phrases, which assign a place so much higher to matters of worship than to habitual duty, is to be attributed to the influence of priestly tradition. They are the result of the sacerdotal spirit, which, during past ages, swayed the thoughts and language of the Christian world. It is one of the natural characteristics of a system of priestly devotion that it ascribes to clerical functions and services a character of holiness superior to that which it gives to the actions of every-day life. A priesthood can maintain its power only by exalting the rites of religious worship to a loftier level than worldly duties. The greater the distinction it makes between the sphere of religion and that of worldly life, the more does it surround the ministerial office and its acts with those imposing associations of sacredness with which it desires to invest them. That the work of the world therefore is, according to familiar forms of language, "secular," while acts of worship are "sacred"; that it is "common" to labour, and "divine service" to pray; that trading and working are "worldly," and devotional services "religious"; that days devoted to ecclesiastical observances are "holy," and time spent in business is not; are traditions of the sacerdotal spirit. They are results which we have derived from the prevalence of the priestly idea that what is ecclesiastical is alone holy; that true piety is in ritual, not in life. The language of the New Testament is as opposite as possible to this. Our "reasonable service"[1] it represents as consisting in presenting ourselves as a living sacrifice to God; and "pure and undefiled religion"[2] it describes as finding its true office in "visiting the fatherless and widows in their affliction, and keeping ourselves unspotted from the world."

"Spiritual." One of the terms which are employed in familiar language to distinguish what belongs to the Church from what pertains to ordinary human life is so significant as to deserve special notice. It is the word "Spiritual." The clergy are, according to this form of current language, "spiritual" persons; their functions are "spiritual"; ecclesiastical government and jurisdiction are also de-

---

[1] Rom. xii. 1.

[2] James i. 27. "Service" and "religion" do not clearly bring out the meaning of the original words, which is rather "worship"; the idea conveyed being that the consecration of the daily life is true Christian worship.

scribed by the same epithet; while "spiritual" independence and "spiritual" authority are claimed as rights belonging to a Christian society. Other men, other things are represented, on the contrary, as "temporal," or "civil," or "secular." Now, here we have another instance of a use assigned to language by priestly tradition, which tends to create a false impression. In appropriating the term "spiritual" to the designation of persons and matters belonging to the ecclesiastical sphere, the assumption was originally involved that they possess a character of sanctity and elevation, which raises them above the province of ordinary human concerns. And, though the word is so often employed as a mere customary epithet that it does not convey in many instances the idea of anything more than an outward distinction, it yet exercises also, in some measure, a misleading influence. It is apt to be overlooked that this ecclesiastical sense of "spiritual" is very different from the elevated meaning which it bears in the New Testament. It is not unnaturally supposed, when a title which has such a lofty signification in Scripture is applied to matters of church polity, that the principle involved in them is of transcendent importance. Ecclesiastical controversialists are fond of employing a word, which serves to give the standing of vital questions to the points for which they contend. It is on "spiritual" grounds that the claims of systems of church government have often been maintained. It is in the lofty character of "spiritual" rights and privileges that articles of church order have very frequently been insisted on, and insisted on with the most fervid zeal. But the word is really, when applied in this way, a misnomer. Questions of the external arrangements and polity of the Church are not spiritual, in the true acceptation of the term. The epithet can only be so employed by wrongly transferring it from things which belong to the inner life and the moral sphere, and applying it to the outward matters of religion. Nothing could show more strikingly the contradiction between the high sense of the word originally, and the lower one which sacerdotal tradition has given to it, than to advert to the instances in church history in which so-called "spiritual" claims and prerogatives have been most zealously maintained. For it has often happened that, while these were being most earnestly contended for, true spirituality had fallen into utter decay.

These examples may serve, in some degree, to illustrate the general fact of the influence which has been exercised by sacerdotalism in impressing its mode of thought and feeling on forms of language. We have only to reflect on the extent to which the traditions of a priestly faith have been spread over the world, and on the length of time during which these existed as almost the sole rule and guide for Christian opinion, in order to see how it has happened, as a matter of course, that they have left their mark on religious phraseology. It could not but occur that the words and phrases of common language should receive their shape and meaning, in no inconsiderable measure, from a power so great and lasting.

II.

It is not less true that those Dogmatic Forms of Religious Thought, which are contained in the creeds and theological systems that have found their way at various times into the Christian Church, have had an important effect on words; and have led more especially to material alterations in the sense of some of the terms which are used in the New Testament.

<small>New Testament language not theological.</small> It should be borne in mind that the language of the New Testament is not that of theological statement. Its terms and its modes of thought are such as belonged to popular usage. The design of the New Testament writers was not to formulate opinion, but to produce living faith, and purity of life; and the phraseology, therefore, which they employed has all the width and freedom of ordinary forms of expression. It was only at a later stage in the history of Christianity that scientific exactness was attempted to be introduced into the statement of religious truth; and, though the change is one which arose naturally in the course of events,[1] it has inevitably had the effect of modifying, to a very considerable extent, the use of Christian terms. To take the thoughts which Christ and the Apostles had expressed popularly and re-cast them in the form of logical propositions, was necessarily to assign elements of meaning to the original words more or less differing from what they at first possessed. It is

---

[1] This is attempted to be shown in the account given in the next chapter of the rise and growth of creeds.

impossible to give to Christianity the shape of a creed, or a theological system, without a measure of change being made from the New Testament sense of words.

We have therefore to take into account the fact that language which in Scripture has a large and popular signification has subsequently been invested, in some cases, with a more formal and exact sense—that a secondary theological meaning has been impressed on a number of words, which were used with a freer and wider meaning at first. Thus an illustration is to be seen in the word "Faith." The ecclesiastical acceptation of that term makes it mean very often nothing more than the recognition of certain articles of belief. The "faith" of the Church is in common language simply its creed. But that formal sense of the term is entirely foreign to the New Testament. It is a signification which has been given to it by theological tradition. While the faith of primitive Christianity involved, no doubt, an intellectual assent to certain facts and views, it was pre-eminently belief in Christ as a personal and living Saviour. A similar change from the New Testament use to the theological point of

"Faith."

view of later times is observable in the word "Doctrine." That term, and its equivalents in the original Greek, signify primarily "instruction" or "teaching," and the reference of the expression at first was by no means to merely theoretical views of religious truth. But, in course of time, the "doctrines" of Christianity have come to represent matters of Christian belief, as distinguished from the duties of Christianity. And the consequence of this alteration in the use of the term is necessarily to lead to a serious misunderstanding of Scripture, unless allowance is made for the change. Anyone, for example, who does not take into account that "doctrine" in the New Testament has the wide, general sense of teaching, and not the modern meaning of abstract belief, is certain to misinterpret St. Paul's allusion to the "form of doctrine" which he declares to have been "delivered" to the Roman Christians.[1] In point of fact it has been inferred from this passage that there were formal articles of belief then in existence. But that is entirely to mistake the meaning of the words. The whole context shows that what

[1] Rom. vi. 17.

the Apostle is referring to is a form of *teaching*, and that the nature of the instruction conveyed by it was such as had to do, not with matters of abstract faith, but with the regulation of the life: it was such that obedience to it " made men free from sin, and the servants of righteousness."[1] So, too, when St. Paul speaks of " sound doctrine," a reader with the modern view of the meaning of the phrase naturally regards it as signifying orthodox belief; but that is not the real sense of the expression. What is meant is sound or wholesome *teaching*—teaching having a healthful, practical tendency.[2]

[1] Id. 18. The true rendering of the passage is given in the Revised Version, " Ye became obedient from the heart to that form of teaching whereunto ye were delivered; and, being made free from sin, ye became servants of righteousness." The meaning is, that they had been delivered to the influence of Christian teaching, as a plastic material is delivered to a mould or pattern to be shaped by it.

[2] It cannot be said that the Revised Version has dealt satisfactorily with this term. The consideration that " doctrine " now very generally signifies, as we have seen, what is quite foreign to New Testament ideas, should have led the Revisers to retain that word, if they retained it at all, only if the context, in any case in which it occurs, is such as clearly to show that it bears the sense of teaching. But it is impossible to make out from the course which they have followed that they have been guided by any

It would be easy to multiply illustrations of the fact that ecclesiastical usage has thus had the effect of altering the sense of a number of the terms of the New Testament from their original use to a more formal and abstract meaning. But the example which affords probably the most striking evidence of this, and which, at the same time, is most suggestive of the altered relation to Christian truth which the Church now holds, as compared with what it originally did, is the term heresy.

'Heresy.' This word, as it has been long understood, and is now understood, denotes deviation from a doctrinal standard. But its signification in the New Testament does not correspond to this idea. "Heresy," as referred to there, denotes, when the term is used in an unfavourable sense,[1] not merely an

consistent principle. In some instances they have substituted "teaching" for "doctrine"; in others they have retained the latter term in the text, and put "teaching" into the margin, without any apparent reason for the difference; while they make St. Paul exhort Timothy to "take heed to his *teaching*" (1 Tim. iv. 16) and Titus to "show uncorruptness in his *doctrine*" (Tit. ii. 7), the word in the two passages being precisely the same in the original.

[1] It is the same term which is used in Acts v. 17; xv. 5, etc., and translated "sect," without any unfavourable meaning being intended.

error of opinion, but of life. Its reference is not merely to speculative views but to moral failings. Thus " the works of the flesh are manifest, which are these, adultery, fornication, uncleanness, lasciviousness, idolatry, witchcraft, hatred, variance, emulations, wrath, strife, seditions, *heresies*, envyings, murders, drunkenness, revellings and such like." [1] It is obvious, both from the epithet " works of the flesh " which is applied to them, and from the nature of the faults along with which they are here classed, that by " heresies " in this passage are meant very much more than mere aberrations from a certain standard of belief. And so also when, in the Corinthian Church, grave abuses arose in connection with the celebration of the Lord's Supper, and St. Paul wrote to the members of that communion, " there must also be heresies among you, that they which are approved may be made manifest among you," [2] the term clearly does not denote false opinions, but offences against the spirit of Christianity, arising from party feeling. The same reference to moral obliquity, rather than to mere intellectual error, is observable in what is said of a

[1] Gal. v. 20.   [2] 1 Cor. xi. 19

heretic, "A man that is an heretic, after a first and second admonition, reject (or avoid); knowing that he that is such is perverted, and sinneth, being condemned of himself."[1] These words describe the "heretic" not merely as heterodox, but as sinful and depraved. It is not less clear that, when St. Peter describes certain false teachers as "bringing in destructive heresies, denying even the Master that bought them, bringing upon themselves swift destruction,"[2] his reference is not so much to the propagation of speculative error as to the dissemination of immoral principles. For these teachers are described by him as "lascivious," "covetous," "having eyes full of adultery, and that cannot cease from sin," and by many similar epithets.

Now the fact that ecclesiastical usage has, in course of time, eliminated from the meaning of the word "heresy" the element of moral evil, and has restricted it to signify merely disagreement with a certain standard of religious opinion, is remarkable and suggestive. In the first place it furnishes a striking instance in proof of the language of the New Testament having been modified

---

[1] Tit. iii. 10.   [2] 2 Peter ii. 1, etc.

in meaning by the influence of the dogmatic treatment of Christian truth. And, therefore, like the other examples which we have given, and like many similar cases which might be added, it shows that any one who desires to interpret the words of Christ and the Apostles in the sense in which they were originally employed, must allow for this source of difference. But there is another and wider lesson which is to be learned, This change in the meaning of the word "heresy" shows the altered position in which the Christian Church now stands to religious truth from that which it at first held. The New Testament writers did not conceive of Christianity as a system of intellectual belief on the one hand, and of practical obligation on the other. They do not deal with it as consisting of matters of faith separately from matters of duty. In their view faith and duty, belief and life are essentially united. It is only as a result of the theological treatment of Christianity, which belongs to later ages, that a formal division has been made between these two elements of Christian truth. And, while we must regard this separation of Christian creed from Christian life, which is a feature of theological statements of religion, as a necessary result of the development of opinion, there can be no doubt that it is a source of grave danger. One of the most frequent, as well as one of the most fatal, errors in the Christian Church has been that of exalting mere orthodoxy above purity of character, and making a man's creed the sole test of his Christianity. The strangest anomalies are often presented in this respect. Sometimes the fervid opponent of what are believed to be unorthodox views is far from being characterized by a scrupulous regard to the moral obligations of religion. Very frequently the course which is taken to repress speculative error is one in which the practical requirements of Christianity are, to a large extent, set aside; and in which zeal for orthodoxy is gratified at the expense of charity and justice. Now, one of the strongest arguments which can be appealed to to show the falseness of this state of sentiment is its utter contrariety to the point of view from which heresy was originally regarded. The "heretic," in apostolic language, is pre-eminently the offender against the spirit and the moral law of Christianity. Whatever errors of belief he may hold, they are errors mingled with wickedness, and tending to wickedness. Mere deviation from an intellectual standard is not what the apostolic writers mean by "heresy." They view faith and life as one and indivisible, and therefore error is regarded by them as falseness of practice, and not merely of belief. It would have been well if this primitive idea of heresy had been adhered to in the Christian Church—if the state of a man's opinions had not been separated so much from that of his moral nature, and the worst deviation from Christianity had been considered to be deviation from it as a law of life.

III.

A third source of error in the use of ecclesiastical phraseology consists in the undue Limitation of Terms—in their being confined to a narrower meaning than is consistent with their original and proper sense. There is often in the history of traditional phrases a restriction of their true signification. They are apt, in course of lengthened use, to lose somewhat of the meaning which they possessed at first; and so to become representative of only a part of the truth

Effect of controversy in narrowing the meaning of terms.

which they at first indicated. And, while this holds in regard to words employed with reference to all subjects, it is especially true of those which have been identified with party conflict. The natural result, when names and phrases are long used in controversy, is that they acquire meanings more limited than they had primarily. The tendency of the supporters of conflicting modes of opinion is to seize on those interpretations of language which lend most encouragement to the particular views for which they contend. It is hardly necessary to point out that ecclesiastical subjects, from the immense amount of keen discussion which they have awakened, have been peculiarly exposed to the influence of this kind of change as regards the meaning of terms.

"Catholic." The use of the term "Catholic," as applied to the Church, is an instance of a phrase descending from a large signification to one of restricted extent. In its true and primary sense it is simply a name for the fact declared by the New Testament that all Christians throughout the world constitute the Church of Christ. But this idea of universality has now been, in great measure, lost from the word; and it is chiefly used to designate one section of Christians.[1]

Another example, which is equally important, *"Schism."* but the evidence of which does not lie so much on the surface, is to be found in the term "Schism." The recognized meaning of this word now is ecclesiastical separation. The sin of "schism" is regarded as consisting in the severance of the Church of Christ—in its rupture into distinct communities. That, however, is a departure from the sense which the word bears in the New Testament. There it means simply, when applied to human conduct, "division," or "dissension," or "strife."[2] In the only instance in which it is used in regard to a church, namely in the case of the Church at Corinth, there had been no external separation; that communion still retained its outward unity;[3] and evidently all that St. Paul means by alluding to "schisms" as

---

[1] An account of the different shades of meaning which have been given to the term "catholic" will be found in Bishop Pearson on the Creed.

[2] John vii. 43, "There was a *division* among the people because of Him"; literally a "schism." So also John ix. 16, and x. 19.

[3] This is evident from the words in which it is addressed, 1 Cor. i. 2.

having a place in it is, that it was disturbed by internal differences.[1] It thus appears that the traditional signification which is now attached to the term, according to which it means outward separations of Christians, is one that has been assigned to it by later usage; and, moreover, it is a change from a larger to a more narrow sense. The apostolic idea of schism, that it is simply religious strife, is a far larger and truer conception than that of the ecclesiastics of subsequent times, who have identified it with external divisions. For true unity is unity of spirit. There may be, as in the Corinthian Church, party contentions of the most bitter character, where there is no outward severance of a Christian society. There may be all the evils of "jealousy and strife,"[2] which are the true evils of division,

---

[1] The words in which the Apostle refers to the "schisms" of the Corinthian Church plainly bear this meaning :—" I beseech you, brethren, by the name of our Lord Jesus Christ, that ye all speak the same thing, and that there be no divisions (literally schisms) among you; but that ye be perfectly joined together in the same mind, and in the same judgment. For it hath been declared unto me of you, my brethren, by them which are of the house of Chloe, that there are contentions among you." 1 Cor. i. 10, 11. So also xi. 18.

[2] 1 Cor. iii. 3.

without any positive breach of external unity. And, on the other hand, it is not less true that between religious communions which are separate there may exist a spirit of amity and peace. So that the real element of sin in ecclesiastical differences—the real evil of schism—is not in the fact of outward separation, but in the existence of strife, which may prevail where there is no separation at all. And, therefore, when St. Paul employs the word "schism" in the sense of "strife," he expresses by it, as we have said, a much larger and more far-reaching idea of the nature of the evil than is represented by the traditional use of the word to mean merely breach of outward unity. Indeed, the effect of this secondary sense, which ecclesiastical usage has given to the term, has been largely that of rendering it a medium of asserting exclusive claims in behalf of each church-party. For nothing is easier than for each section of professing Christians to accuse those who are apart from it of separating from the true communion of Christ. And we find consequently that this has been done by almost every side. The Greek Church regards the Church of Rome as schismatic, and the same charge is made by the Church of Rome against the Greek Church. Protestants are considered by the Church of Rome to be in a state of schism, and the same accusation is brought by some Protestants against others. Thus "schism," in the ecclesiastical sense of separation, can readily be charged by any society of Christians against those who do not belong to it; because if it claims to be the only true Church of Christ, it will also view all who are outside its limits as being wanderers from the divine fold. The history of the Church, in short, shows that "schism" has been pretty much a charge made by every church-party in turn against those who are in a state of separation from itself. On the contrary, the apostolic use of the term, according to which it denotes the fact of strife and contention, directs us to that which is the real evil of religious differences, and which is chargeable more or less against every party.[1]

---

[1] The Revised Version is chargeable with as great want of consistency in its treatment of this word as we noticed in connection with its use of the term doctrine. While it gives "divisions" as the English of the word in the 1st and 11th chapters of 1 Corinthians, it follows the Authorized Version in unjustifiably changing the translation to

We may also class under this head another phrase, which has been employed very frequently in connection with ecclesiastical questions; but often, as it seems to us, without keeping in view its original and full meaning. The Scriptural designation of Christ as "Head of the Church" has been largely imported into the discussion of matters of church government. Especially has this been the case in connection with Presbyterian views of church government. Anyone who looks into the Presbyterian treatises belonging to the seventeenth century, which deal with questions of ecclesiastical polity, will find very frequent references to Christ's Sovereignty and Headship in relation to His Church; and he will find that many of the views which were entertained by the Presbyterian divines of that age, as regards church matters, were founded on their beliefs with reference to this subject. And the doctrine of the "Headship of Christ," which was elaborated at that period, has become part of the

Christ the "Head of the Church."

" schism " in 1 Cor. xii. 25, instead of keeping to the same rendering throughout. Not only so, but it fails even to adopt the precaution in regard to this latter passage which the Authorized Version does: for *it* inserts "division" in the margin, which the Revisers have omitted.

traditional equipment of Presbyterianism. It still mingles in its accustomed phraseology, and is appealed to as constituting a principle which is characteristic of its system. It may well be questioned, however, whether, in employing the New Testament representation of Christ as being "Head of the Church" as a ground for arguing points of ecclesiastical government, an interpretation has not been applied to New Testament language, which is inconsistent with its real meaning—whether the sense of the phrase has not been narrowed to support what is remote from its true intention. What is the real sense in which St. Paul describes Christ as sustaining this relation?[1] The idea implied plainly is, that the union of Christ with His people is similar to the connection of the head with the members of the body—that He is the origin, and also the ruling and sustaining power, as regards the spiritual life of His people; while they, on their part, are one with Him in faith and love. But the language manifestly applies to a spiritual fact. It seems altogether inconsistent with the Apostle's meaning to suppose that he intended

[1] Eph. iv. 15; Col. i. 18; &c.

to represent that Christ is the Head of an ecclesiastical incorporation, or that he was referring to matters of church-polity at all. What, on the other hand, he clearly designs to teach is that Christ is the spiritual life and strength of all Christians— of all who believe in and serve Him. And the explanation of the fact that this phrase of the New Testament, which really has nothing to do with questions as to forms of ecclesiastical polity, has been nevertheless introduced so largely into the discussion of them, is to be found, we believe, in a circumstance to which we have already alluded. We have seen in a previous chapter that, in the seventeenth century, notions which have their proper place in the system of the Old Testament were largely applied to the settlement of points relating to the Christian Church.[1] It was attempted to model everything according to Jewish ideas. The predominant aim of the Presbyterians of the age was to establish a theocracy analogous to the Jewish system of government, and they regarded Christ as Sovereign and Ruler of the Church in the same sense as Jehovah had been of ancient

[1] See pp. 101, etc.

Israel.[1] The effect was that they unconsciously coloured with this view the statements of the New Testament; and it led them to assign to the assertion that Christ is the Head of the Church a meaning which is quite alien from the Apostle's intention. Nor is this misappropriation of a Scripture phrase exempt from danger. It tends to exalt the special features of a form of church-government far above their true value. That Christ is the Head of all faithful souls everywhere is a great and wholesome spiritual truth, which deserves to be held as of the highest importance. That He is the Head specially of a Presbyterian communion, or of any other ecclesiastical society in particular, is a wholly different and unwarranted allegation. And, moreover, it is a belief which necessarily leads to

---

[1] "The General Assembly was the governing body of Scotland, and its ministers and elders constantly declared that they had derived their legislative authority from Jesus Christ, the King and Head of His Church. Never since the Jewish theocracy was dissolved had such a spectacle been seen. The Old Testament epoch seemed to have been revived in our country. Even the wars were religious wars; and this was proved by the fact that in the Old Testament the wars of God's people were called the wars of the Lord." Cunningham's Church History of Scotland. Year 1643.

exclusive pretension and bigotry. For, if we entertain the idea that the Lord Jesus Christ occupies, in relation to the particular Christian society to which we belong, the position of Divine Head, while other Christians do not stand in the same connection with Him, this is a view which involves substantially the same kind of claim to the sole possession of God's favour as is held by the most extreme sacerdotalist.

We have already had occasion to point out that the dogma of the "Visible Church" has held a prominent part in the formation of certain ecclesiastical views, and that its tendency has been in the direction of a narrow idea of the Christian Church. This is another instance of a phrase becoming dissociated from its primary use, and taking on it a different and more restricted meaning. It was originally part of the distinction, which was introduced, in the early days of Protestantism, between the Church visible, and the Church invisible. The object of this distinction was to denote the difference between the existing imperfect condition of the communion of Christians, and its ideal and ultimate state. In the one aspect, the Church

The "Visible Church."

was designated as "visible," because it is such as appears to human perception; in the other, it was characterized as "invisible," because it is the true and final condition of the Church known only to God himself.[1] Whatever may be thought of the phraseology in which this distinction was thus expressed, there can be no doubt of the importance of the fact which it represents. For one of the worst sources of confusion and controversy in the history of the Church has been the failure to distinguish

---

[1] We find the elements, at least, of this distinction as far back as in Zwingle's Confession presented to the Emperor Charles V. in 1530. He speaks, on the one hand, of the Church of the elect known to God alone; and, on the other, of the Church discernible by the human senses, which consists of all who make profession of Christ, including wicked as well as good persons. The Second Helvetic Confession, of a somewhat later date, also contains an approximation to it. "God has," it says, "in this world, and amidst these shadows, those who are His own true worshippers; for the Apostle exclaims, the foundation of God standeth sure, having this seal, the Lord knoweth them that are His. Whence the Church may be called invisible, not because the men are invisible of whom the Church is composed, but because, hidden from our eyes, but known to God alone, it often eludes human judgment. On the other hand, not all who are reckoned as in the Church are holy, and living, and true members of the Church: for there are many hypocrites."

between its actual and its ideal conditions; and the mistake, in consequence, of insisting that a standard of purity is to be reached by it, which in present circumstances is unattainable.[1] The account which we have elsewhere given, however, of the use of the term "Visible Church" shows that it became disconnected to a large extent from this its original intention, and came to be identified with the maintenance of those predominantly external conceptions of the Church, which have tended so much to supersede large and spiritual views of its nature and extent.[2]

Such are some instances in which the phraseology employed with reference to subjects connected with the Christian Church is apt to convey misconception and error. We have seen that, alike in connection with its ministry, its worship, its faith, and its government, not a few of those terms which have established themselves in frequent use are liable to be attended with considerable misapprehension. The illustrations we have adduced are not intended to afford more than a very imperfect elucidation of a subject

Conclusion.

---

[1] This subject is treated in Chapter VII. [2] See p. 25.

which is capable of much more extensive treatment. The preceding discussion, however, will have its use, if it helps to show the influence of words in relation to ecclesiastical questions; and if it exemplifies the danger of their misapplication, and the need of receiving merely traditional meanings and forms of language with caution. Such elements of error connected with the use of words as we have pointed out in the preceding observations˙ are, for the most part, associated with lengthened usage. They are therefore the more apt to be accepted without question. But the careful inquirer will not be content to take expressions as correct simply because they have the sanction of long-continued use; and he will especially examine with care whether terms which are derived from Scripture, and which are employed as having its authority, are applied according to their real and primary sense.

CHAPTER VI.

CREEDS.

"It hath pleased God that all things on earth should bear the marks of a state of imperfection; imperfect human persons are the penmen of religious truth; and imperfect human language is the conveying part of the matter; and the method and phrase, though they may be true and blameless, are far short of the heavenly perfection."—RICHARD BAXTER.

CREEDS.

<small>*A creed a natural provision in a Christian society.*</small>

ALTHOUGH the subject of creeds is one which, in the actual history of Christianity, has been attended with great difficulties, the employment of a form of religious belief is in itself an obvious and natural provision. Association for religious purposes necessarily implies agreement in reference to matters of religious faith. Christian communion and co-operation cannot exist except on the basis of a common Christian profession. That those who unite, therefore, as members of the same religious body, in acts of mutual service and common worship, should have some recognized expression of their consent in matters of belief, seems only natural and reasonable.

It is necessary to advert to this general aspect

of the question of creeds, because, in the controversies which have been carried on in regard to them, the position sometimes taken up is that of uncompromising antagonism to all creeds. The true solution of the problems attending them lies, it is urged, in their entire disuse. If confessions and symbols of Christian belief were done away altogether, the intellectual freedom which is the proper possession of religious thought, would, it is maintained, be secured, and Christianity would then unfold itself healthily and vigorously. At present—is the argument of those who support this view—the truth is hindered and restricted by formal articles of faith, and to liberate it from such restraints is necessary in order to restore its purity and power.

How the demand for a creed arises.

But, whatever may be the evils connected with creeds, the general principle which they involve seems quite a reasonable one. If a religious society implies, as one of the conditions of its existence, a common understanding in regard to matters of faith, it follows that to *express* that understanding in a more or less definite form is not only allowable, but may in certain circumstances be necessary. Let us suppose that a number of professing Christians associate together for purposes of instruction and worship without having any formal agreement as regards the tenets they maintain. Even in that case a common consent to certain beliefs, however vague, is necessarily involved. Were they not avowedly at one in regard to certain primary elements of Christianity, they could not associate for the ends of Christian worship and teaching. Now, it is quite possible that a community of Christians may exist for a time without having any urgent reason for giving explicit shape to the sense of agreement which thus unites them. Their experience of the practical power of Christianity may be so strong, and their activity in the performance of its duties so absorbing, as to throw questions of opinion entirely into the background. The *feeling* of harmony among them may be sufficiently powerful and continuous to enable them to dispense with *literal terms* of agreement. But the usual course of human experience forbids us to expect that such a state of things will last indefinitely. Diversity of views sooner or later asserts itself in every society, and renders it advisable that there should be a common standard to which appeal may be made. Hence, although at first, and for a time, Christian people may be able to join together in worship, and to co-operate for Christian ends, without having anything more than a vague, undefined understanding in regard to the points of their common belief, it is obvious that the natural tendency of events at a later stage of their history will be in a different direction; that, with the introduction of controversy, and the awakening of doubts and intellectual difficulties, it will become a measure of expediency or necessity to lay down a definite statement of the elements of their faith.

No sufficient reason against a creed that there is no formulary of belief in the New Testament.

A creed is therefore the fulfilment of a demand naturally arising in the history of religion. Nor is it a sufficient objection to formularies of belief to say that no creed is to be found in the New Testament. The absence of systematic articles of faith from the New Testament writings is, no doubt, a significant fact; and an important inference may be regarded as being suggested by this omission;[1] but it by no means proves that they

---

[1] This subject is considered by Archbishop Whately in his Essay on the Omission of Articles of Faith in the New Testament. His argument is that this omission is a proof of the wisdom by which the writers of the New Testament

are inadmissible, or in all circumstances unnecessary. The most that can be asserted with truth as being shown by this omission is, that no creed, in the strictly technical sense of the term, existed in the primitive age of Christianity. But it would be utterly incorrect to suppose that communion with the Christian Church did not from the first involve the acceptance of certain positive beliefs, though these had not yet been moulded into a formal declaration of faith. Nothing can be clearer than that the fellowship of the primitive Christians was based upon their common belief in the great distinctive facts of Christ's history and mission—His advent in the flesh, the crucifixion, the resurrection, His glorified life, and His second coming. That such primary matters of faith were not, in the earliest period of Christianity, put into the form of a systematic statement of belief cannot be justly held as a reason why this should never be done. The circum-

---

were guided; as the insertion of a fixed creed in Scripture for all future times would have been inconsistent with the requirements of the Church, no one formulary of faith being applicable to all the varying conditions of religious truth. Essays on some of the Peculiarities of the Christian Religion. First Series.

stances which existed in the first age of the Church were so different from those of following times that no conclusion of this kind is justified. We know that, in the period succeeding that of the Apostles, there was a distinctly marked change in the direction of more logical and systematic definition of religious truth. What is called the Apostles' Creed was in use—at least in substance—not long after their time. In the early Christian centuries other formularies of the Christian faith were added. That the efforts which were put forth in this direction in the times succeeding the Apostolic Age were often misapplied; that, in the strife about mere terms and definitions, the life and power of religion were frequently lost sight of, there can be no doubt. At the same time it may be fairly argued that these were but the abuses arising out of a change which was in itself natural and unavoidable. For the condition of things which arose, after the exceptional influences that attended the birth and infancy of the Church had passed away, was such as necessarily to suggest the formation of a settled creed. Religious speculation diverged so widely from the faith which had been handed down from Christ and the Apostles, that the desire was naturally created for a formal statement of the chief elements of Christianity. It was only by this means that those who cherished the primitive beliefs of the Church could maintain a distinction between them, and other opinions with which they were in danger of being identified.

Thus the introduction of creeds into the Christian Church presents a close analogy to the rise and growth of other elements of ecclesiastical order. There are three constituents which enter into the social constitution of the Church—its common rule or discipline, its common worship, and its common faith. Each of these, existing only in a general form during the earliest age of Christianity, gradually assumed a more definite and established shape as time advanced. The common rule or discipline of Christians became developed into settled church government. Common worship grew during the post-apostolic period into a recognized and detailed ritual. And it is evident that the same law of change could not but exercise its influence also as regards the faith of the Church. So that the introduction of creeds only

Analogy between development of creeds and that of other elements of church order.

exemplifies the operation of a principle which has extended its agency to every one of the constituent elements of church-order. As the common rule or discipline of Christians came to embody itself in modes of ecclesiastical government, as their common worship found expression in ritual, so the common Christian faith assumed an external shape in creeds.

We may accept then, it seems to us, the existence of creeds as a fact of religion which is in accordance with the natural growth and history of faith.[1] Nor does it appear, when we examine in detail the chief objections usually brought

---

[1] Though we speak of the existence of creeds as being connected with the natural growth and history of faith, it is not implied that they constitute an advance on primitive Christian teaching. On the contrary, while the scientific treatment of Christianity, and its formation into theological systems have answered certain important purposes, and are processes which accord with the ordinary exercise of the reason, the living and practical teaching of the New Testament is of a higher character than theological forms. Some of the statements in Swainson's Hulsean Lectures on the Creeds of the Church seem to be open to objection from this point of view. His suggestive and interesting remarks on the progressive unfolding of divine truth throughout the Christian ages assign a value to creeds, in connection with the fuller manifestation of truth, which may be questioned.

against them, that these objections prove anything more than the liability of forms of faith, like all other religious forms, to be misunderstood and misused.

Thus the objection to creeds on the ground of their *formal and dogmatic treatment of religious truth* is not one that can reasonably be entertained. For the reduction of the truths of religion to systematic order is a process which is quite in accordance with the course we naturally pursue in all intellectual research. When we carefully study any subject, we necessarily seek to bring it into a definite form. We analyze and classify its various parts. We set ourselves to discover the abstract principles which it involves, and the relations which it bears to other elements of knowledge. In short, all examination of truth requires the use of methodical processes, and of abstract modes of statement. And therefore, when this treatment is applied to religious truth, it is only following out the same line of inquiry and of procedure as we employ in reference to other subjects of thought. Dogma—meaning by that term the doctrinal treatment of religion—is simply the application to this de-

[marginal note: First objection to creeds—their formal treatment of religious truth.]

partment of truth of the scientific method which is used in the investigation of other branches of knowledge. For example, suppose we desire to understand the nature of the teachings of Scripture on the subject of the death of Christ for sin. In order to arrive at an exact conclusion with reference to it, the inquiry we make must embrace various particulars. For instance, we must compare one statement of Scripture with another, we must also endeavour to ascertain the general principles which are implied in these statements, and we must direct our efforts to the discovery of the relations in which this truth stands to others. The result of this process is the formation of a certain theory, which we reach as a deduction from all these particulars taken together. We speak of a theory so arrived at in regard to the death of Christ for sin as representing "the doctrine of the atonement," while this mode of dealing with religious truth is, in technical language, "theology." But, in point of fact, this intellectual method is neither more nor less than that which is followed in the intelligent investigation of any kind of truth. By a necessity of our mental nature we seek to formulate the results of thought in regard to religion, as in regard to any other subject. We endeavour instinctively to systematize our conclusions, so as to form them into one whole. So that dogmatic forms of religious thought are really the development of a course of mental effort which is perfectly natural.

And therefore it is that creeds and theological systems are to be found in connection with every phase of Christianity. Men will endeavour—in spite of all that may be urged against the formulation of belief—to give definite shape to their religious views.[1] It consists with the

[1] Even in religious societies where we would least expect systematic articles of faith to find a place they have in some form or another been adopted. Thus the Unitarians, considering the position of antagonism to received dogmas which they usually assume, and the almost unqualified latitude which they give to religious thought, might be expected entirely to repudiate everything like formal articles of belief ; but even Unitarianism has had its creed. Theodore Parker's Works, vol. i. 311. For reasons of a different character, it might well be considered in the highest degree improbable that the Society of Friends, or Quakers, should have a creed. Their strong sentiments as regards the superiority of religion to forms, and their views in reference to the communication of truth by the direct agency of the Spirit, render it an anomaly that they should formulate their beliefs.

natural tendencies of thought to do so. No doubt, most serious evils have arisen in connection with dogmatic conceptions and statements of religious truth. Intolerance has ever found one of its most effectual weapons in the articles of a creed. Phrases and propositions are often exalted into essential tests of Christian truth, while the spirit of Christianity is neglected. But it should be borne in mind that forms of faith are only attended in this respect with the same danger, which, as we have said, is associated with religious forms in general. Thus the rites and observances of Christian worship are connected, in the history of the Church, with many corruptions. So also much of the strife, and bitterness, and wrong existing in the Christian world is traceable to the fanatical zeal with

Yet Barclay's Apology is really a confession of the Quaker faith; and, although his preface refers unfavourably to human learning, and reflects severely on "school divinity," there is a strong flavour of both in the contents of the document. Witness this, for example, "Seeing we do therefore receive and believe the Scriptures, because they proceeded from the Spirit, therefore, also, the Spirit is more originally and principally the rule, according to that received maxim in the schools, *That for which a thing is such, that thing itself is more such.*"

which modes of church government have been confounded with the essence of Christianity. These, however, in common with the intolerance which has so often been characteristic of the use of creeds, are but evils which will arise when the formal matters of religion are concerned. They are instances of the *misuse* of the formal —of its being over-estimated and magnified, at the expense of the higher and spiritual elements of faith.

The common objection, also, that creeds are *inconsistent with the exercise of independent thought,* can only be admitted to apply to an evil which is incidental to them, and is not a charge which holds against them essentially. For, admitting that the exercise of the individual judgment is often sacrificed to an undue regard for forms of belief, there is yet a useful function which they are fitted to serve quite compatible with the right of each man to think for himself in matters of religion. It is argued by those who are opposed on this ground to confessions and systems of faith, that they were constructed, for the most part, in times long gone by, that they are handed down from generation to generation invested with

Second objection to creeds—their inconsistency with independent thought.

a merely traditional authority, and that consequently they are accepted to a large extent without any intelligent examination of their contents. There is thus practically, it is said, but little personal investigation of truth on the part of the great majority of Christians. They believe what their forefathers believed, and because they believed it. Instead of inquiring for himself; instead of "proving all things, and holding fast that which is good"; each professing believer receives as true merely what the sanction of past ages has transmitted to him. But, while there is too much truth in the charge that religious beliefs are often accepted blindly on trust, there is another aspect of the matter, which the zealous advocate of independent thought is apt to overlook. He is apt to forget that the wisdom of former ages supplies the foundation of our present attainments—that the investigation of truth must, if it is to be successful, proceed on a knowledge of past results. Though the Reformers asserted strongly the right of private judgment, they were very far from disparaging the teachings of bygone times. They did not hold the right of private judgment in any such sense as that every man must initiate and carry out a process of inquiry for himself, without any regard for what others have thought. On the contrary, they assigned great importance to the forms of belief which have come down from the early Christian centuries.[1] They referred with respect to those writings "which show in what manner, from time to time, the Holy Scriptures have been understood, and explained in the Church of God by the doctors who then lived,"[2] at the same time that they declared that these writings are inferior to Holy Scripture itself. Nor did they scruple to appeal for confirmation of their views to the testimony of the Christian fathers.[3] They thus affirmed the important fact that, though the rights of the individual judgment must be made good as against all pretensions to authority over it, this does not involve a depreciation of the faith and opinions of those who have lived before us; one of the chief duties implied in the exercise of the individual

---

[1] The Formula of Concord, 1576, prepared by several of the leading Protestant divines in the period succeeding that of Luther and Melanchthon, with the design of settling certain controversies.

[2] Id. [3] Id.

judgment being to gain what it can from those sources of guidance which are contributed by the past.

If it is a fatal exaggeration of the value of traditional forms of faith to appeal to them as an infallible authority, it is a hardly less serious mistake to ignore their importance. Notwithstanding the evils that have arisen from tradition, it has a true office to fulfil in relation to religious truth. The opinions of the great minds of former days, and the results arrived at by the wisdom of the past, constitute an element of immense value for our guidance in the highest knowledge. The religious inquirer is not prosecuting a journey over untrodden ground. The subjects which occupy his thoughts have been diligently studied and carefully stated by those who have preceded him; and he takes the best way to reach an enlightened acquaintance with truth, when he makes use of the fruits of their judgment.

Third objection to creeds— their inconsistency with the freedom of a church. Nor can the oft-repeated charge against forms of belief that they are *irreconcilable with the freedom of a Christian society*, and that their abolition would lead to fuller life and liberty, be accepted as well-founded. A very inadequate view is taken of the subject, when it is supposed that to dispense with a definite creed is at all a security for spiritual freedom. The testimony of experience rather goes to show that, in a religious communion from which forms of faith are as far as possible excluded, there may be no such results in the direction of liberty as are so often predicted. Intolerance is not got rid of by getting rid of articles of faith. Indeed, it is not difficult to see that the very absence of an understood bond of common belief from a religious society is necessarily attended with the danger of leading to a state of things very far removed from freedom. For where there is no recognized standard of belief, and opinion is consequently left to develop itself without any unity, dissension and faction must always be apt to gain the ascendency, and so to extinguish freedom. It is very often in this way that what is supposed to be liberty is found to be in reality the very opposite. We throw aside reasonable restrictions under the belief that we are thus to be made more free, and discover that the sole result is to bring ourselves into bondage. While there is an obvious liability of creeds to be made instruments of oppression, it is therefore well to look at the dangers which attend the alternative of their abrogation. The assailant of determinate forms of faith, who promises to liberate the Christian Church from intellectual slavery by their removal, overlooks the peril that lies on the other side. What is found to be true in social life as regards the enjoyment of liberty may be taken as holding good also in the Church. We know that, in the sphere of ordinary social existence, freedom is really possessed only where there are settled conditions for its exercise. The absolute and entire removal of all limitations would not make men more free as members of society, but would destroy true liberty. This principle applies also ecclesiastically. The greatest amount of practical freedom of religious life and thought may be fairly claimed for the religious society which holds with wise moderation a definite form of faith, not for that which seeks to dispense with all definite tenets.

Proper function of creeds.

We have thus endeavoured to show that the existence of creeds has its foundation in the conditions essentially belonging to a Christian society; and moreover that the chief objections which are brought against them apply, rather to the abuses with which they have been attended, than to the principle which they involve. But there remains for consideration the further subject of the place and function of creeds as regards their actual use in the Church, more especially in relation to the question of the nature and extent of their obligation, and by what rule consequently they should be enforced.

Not a little of the difficulty which has arisen in reference to this subject is due to the failure to distinguish sufficiently between two very different conceptions of the nature and authority of creeds. On the one hand, there are those whose theory of unity of belief is so rigid that it requires nothing less than absolute agreement in regard to all doctrinal points. They regard any deviation from a certain exact standard of religious opinion as being necessarily precluded by the association of Christians on the basis of a common faith. On the other hand, it is held by many that all that can be reasonably demanded in a Christian society is, that there should be essential concurrence of

Two different views.

opinion. They urge that entire uniformity of belief is impossible where there is intellectual activity, and that every age must be expected to exercise its own special influences on religious thought. Now, these two widely different views involve, as we have said, different judgments with respect to the nature and the legitimate claims of forms of belief. In the Church of Rome, and in any church which holds the same extreme sacerdotal principles, the former is, as a matter of course, the light in which creeds are regarded; the symbols of belief accepted by them are accepted as in every point divine and authoritative; they are considered to be the infallible decrees of a priesthood inspired by the wisdom of God, and therefore as inferring universal and absolute obligation. The place assigned by Protestant opinion to creeds is very different. It views them as occupying other and lower ground, —as being entirely subordinate to Holy Scripture, which it maintains to be the sole rule of faith and life. And therefore the tendency of Protestant opinion as regards creeds is naturally and necessarily in the direction of the second, and less rigid, conception of their place and functions.

We say that the natural tendency of Protestant ideas is towards a qualified view of the claims of formularies of belief; because it is a fundamental article of Protestantism that the Scriptures alone are the rule of faith and manners, and that no other writings are to be placed on the same level with them. We do not affirm, however, that this is the view which has always, in point of fact, been maintained by Protestants. On the contrary, they have often exalted articles of belief to a position which is essentially inconsistent with the supremacy of Scripture. Accordance with a theological system, not conformity to the Scriptures themselves, has very frequently been the test by which they have judged of the truth or falsehood of religious opinion. And the argument which is adduced for thus assigning to a creed a place of paramount authority is this, that, being a compilation of doctrines formed from Scripture, it is entitled to be received as conveying the sense of the Old and New Testaments, and so as authoritatively expressing the divine mind. That, if we mistake not, is substantially the view of those Protestants who adopt the extremely rigid view of creeds. They hold that

The Protestant view of creeds a qualified one.

Scripture is the only divine rule, but that their creed is merely Scripture in another shape,—Scripture moulded into formal articles of faith; and that therefore it has all the truth and importance that belong to the Word of God. But, plausible as this argument may be, nothing can be more certain than that it is inconsistent with the authentic teaching of the Reformed Churches. That teaching expressly or indirectly repudiates all pretension on behalf of creeds and confessions to exemption from error: it asserts that no human interpretation of Scripture is to be taken as authoritative, and that Scripture, and not any other source whatever, is to be held as the judge of human belief and life.

This shown by the testimony of Protestant Confessions. Thus the Confession of Augsburg[1] says, "In these articles above written, in which is our Confession, is seen a summary of the doctrine of those who teach among us"; and it adds, "If anything is lacking in this Confession, we are prepared, God willing, to present ampler information in accordance with the Scriptures." No words could express more plainly the conviction that this formu-

---

[1] The authors and dates of this Confession and of those two next referred to will be found at pp. 22, 23.

lary of Christian faith was quite subordinate to Scripture; and, moreover, that it was not, and could not claim to be, free from imperfection. All the Protestant Confessions accord in this respect with this the oldest of the symbols of the Reformed Faith. In some of them the modes of expression that are made use of to indicate the absence of all pretension to freedom from defect are very out-spoken. Thus the Confession of Basle declares, "We submit this our Confession to the judgment of sacred Scripture: and we promise that, if we shall be better instructed out of the said Scriptures, we shall always submit to God, and His sacred Word." The Second Helvetic Confession says, "We protest above all things that we are most ready to explain more fully all and each the things here set forth by us, if any one demands it; and to yield and submit in the Lord, not without thanks, to such as may teach us better things out of the Word of God." The ancient Scottish Confession [1] contains a similar avowal, "Protesting that, gif any man will note in this oure Confessioun any article or sentence repugning to God's Holie Word, that it

[1] See p. 130.

wad pleis him of his gentilnes and for Christian cherities saik, to admoneis us of the samyn in writt; and we of our honour and fidelitie do promeis unto him satisfactioun fra the mouth of God (that is, fra His Holy Scriptures) or ellis reformation of that quhilk he sall prove to be amyss."

<small>Further proof from Protestant Confessions.</small> That the Reformers and earliest exponents of Protestant views entertained a qualified estimate of the claims of formularies of belief is manifest from such explicit statements as these. It is evident that they made an essential distinction between them and the Scriptures. It is also plain that they did not challenge for them inherent authority, or completeness, or absolute truth. And those Protestant Confessions which do not, like the formularies we have quoted, contain an express disclaimer of all pretension to freedom from error, declare nevertheless the same thing with equal plainness by the doctrine which they lay down in reference to Scripture. Thus the Westminster Confession is emphatic in asserting the truth and authority of Scripture in contrast to all other opinions and writings whatsoever. It declares that "the Supreme Judge, by which all

controversies of religion are to be determined, and all decrees of councils, opinions of ancient writers, doctrines of men, and private spirits are to be examined, and in whose sentence we are to rest, can be no other but the Holy Spirit speaking in the Scripture."[1] So far from coinciding with the view of those who are disposed to assert that a creed, being an expression of Scripture truth, is entitled to be regarded as equivalent to the sacred writings, it affirms that Scripture must be allowed to be its own interpreter: "the infallible rule of interpretation of Scripture," it says, "is the Scripture itself."[2] Nor is the Westminster Confession content thus to vindicate the sole authority of Scripture, and the unlawfulness of attempting to bind men by any interpretation of its contents; but it also guards against the assumption that any body of men since the Apostles' times has had the right of imposing its decisions as a rule on the Christian Church, and it affirms that no such decisions are to be received except to a modified extent. "All synods or councils since the Apostles' times, whether general or particular, may err, and many have erred; therefore they

[1] Chap. i. section x.   [2] Id. section ix.

are not to be made the rule of faith or practice, but to be used as an help in both."[1]

Twofold nature of the Protestant principle as regards creeds.

Looking therefore at the relation of Protestantism to creeds, in the only light which serves to give us authentic knowledge on the subject—the light afforded by Protestant Confessions themselves—the principle which, as it seems to us, they involve is of a twofold nature. In the first place, the view of a creed which they imply is, that it is a formal expression of agreement in matters of faith. It is impossible, as was remarked at the commencement of this chapter, for a communion of Christians to exist without some consent, understood or explicitly stated, as regards points of belief. Such an understanding or express statement is therefore the fulfilment of a natural want. It represents the common faith of a Christian Society. The Protestant view of the function of creeds does not, however, go farther than this; it does not recognize them as being invested with divine authority, or as being decisive and ultimate expressions of religious truth. On the contrary, there is, in the second place, an element of qualification, according to the Protest-

[1] Chap. xxxi. section iii.

ant opinion, which affects the position of creeds in an important degree. For it holds that they are inferior to Scripture, and cannot rightfully claim to be free from error and defect. Scripture, it maintains, is the sole rule of faith and life. Consequently, the Protestant does not assent to a creed—if he truly holds the principles he professes—in the same way as a member of the Church of Rome, or any other believer in infallible ecclesiastical dogmas. He regards forms of belief as subordinate to the teachings of Scripture, and it is to these last that he looks as his authoritative guide in religious matters. He can accept a creed as nothing more than an imperfect representation of truth, however truly he may accord his adherence to its teachings; because it is a fundamental article of Protestant belief, as embodied in its Confessions, that other writings than Scripture are to be accepted only in this sense.

The conclusion appears to us to follow naturally and of necessity from what we have now described as the Protestant view of creeds, that absolute sameness of belief cannot be insisted on consistently with that view. A church, whose formulary of faith professes to be inferior to Scripture, and

Absolute uniformity of belief not a requirement of the Protestant view.

disavows all claim to unerring certainty, cannot justifiably require that there shall be the same rigid identity of sentiment among its members as it might if it asserted for its articles the character of divine and infallible decrees. The only course reconcilable with the subordinate position thus assumed by a creed is, that its terms should be interpreted and enforced with a width and tolerance, which are in conformity with the character it claims for itself. A statement of religious truth, which declares its own fallibleness and imperfection, cannot reasonably be regarded and enforced as if it were infallible or perfect. The very moderation of its own account of its nature and claims constitutes the strongest possible reason why it should be understood and used with moderation, instead of being made an instrument of undue stringency. It is indeed perfectly true that there are limits beyond which it is unsafe to permit latitude of opinion in a religious communion; and we shall endeavour to indicate further on how the extent to which diversity of opinion is to be allowed can alone be determined. But the point which, in the meantime, we urge as a necessary deduction from the principles which are characteristic of the creeds of Protestantism is, that the rigour that would suppress all differences of thought—the dogmatism that would allow nothing for the exercise of the individual judgment, and that would compel all the members of a Church to think absolutely the same thing, however strongly it is warranted by the doctrine of the infallibilist, is contrary to the view of Protestantism.

And it is really only in this modified use of creeds that the conditions of true unity of belief are to be found. There can be no living unity of belief unless there exists along with it an allowance for diversities of thought. The rigid control of religious faith, which endeavours to prevent all variations from an absolute standard, is fatal to the spiritual condition of a Church. It attempts to create perfect accordance of sentiment by extinguishing intellectual life. It seeks to make men united by destroying individuality of conviction and feeling. Such a system of exaction as regards matters of faith has the effect of crushing out true spiritual energy and mental vitality. On the other hand, when a Church accords a wise latitude in respect of forms of

True unity of faith involves diversity of thought.

P

opinion, though certain evils and disadvantages may arise from the freedom it gives, there are strong counter-balancing elements of good. That religious opinion should flow in a single narrow course is never beneficial. It is in the combination rather of various phases of thought, in the inter-action of contrasting tendencies of belief, that the fullest development of truth is to be sought. The very extremes of opinion, though themselves false, involve important truth; and they can in many cases be most effectually met, not by a mere denial of their accuracy, but by recognizing and employing what in them is good and well-founded. Thus the highest and truest conception of unity of belief is that which associates it with liberty,—that which regards it as many-sided. A dead sameness of faith does not deserve the name of unity of faith. There must be freedom where there is true unity.

Limits to latitude of opinion how to be determined.

But assuming this to be true, and supposing further that we are right in our argument that the position claimed by Protestantism for creeds is in favour of this wide view; it is still indubitable, as we have already observed, that there are limits to the latitude of opinion, which it is safe to permit in a Christian society. The question therefore arises,—How far is diversity of thought admissible? Where is the line to be drawn? Now, the true answer to this question is, we believe, to be found in the function, which has been pointed out as—according to the Protestant conception—belonging to creeds; the function of serving as expressions of the common faith of a Church, and so maintaining a Church in a state of unity in this respect. It follows from this conception of the use of a creed that its function is really administrative. It is an instrument for the preservation of ecclesiastical order. The Christian society itself, therefore, whose form of belief is concerned, must determine, as actual circumstances arise requiring its decision, the extent of the latitude embraced within its communion, and at what point the limits permissible to religious opinion are overpassed. To lay down exact laws on the subject is utterly impracticable. We might as well think of laying down hard and fast rules in reference to any of the complicated problems of ordinary social life. That power belongs of right to a Church

Function of a creed administrative.

to exclude from its communion those who maintain opinions destructive of its welfare seems too obvious to be doubted. But it appears not less clear that the mode in which that power is exercised,—whether wisely or unwisely, whether for good or for evil,—must depend on the religious body itself. A Church that would wisely solve the question of creeds has a general problem to deal with, which does not admit of being settled by regulation, but which requires the exercise of a careful regard to what is most for the good of its members, and the advancement of truth. There are instances in which modes of opinion, even though they may be objectionable, are likely only to assume increased importance by being made the subject of judicial censure. There are other instances in which divergence from the understood tenets of a Christian society may be attended with such manifest practical evils, that their existence demands that action should be taken in reference to them. Ecclesiastical history bears emphatic evidence that, in the past, Churches have erred very much more on the side of severity in this respect than on that of laxity. Both extremes are attended with evil. While order has to be maintained, despotism has to be no less earnestly and carefully avoided. The exercise of the individual Christian judgment cannot be unduly interfered with without an ultimate sacrifice of the interests of the Christian community as a whole. It is obvious, therefore, that a problem so difficult and complicated is only to be solved by the wisdom and moderation, that will be guided by a regard to circumstances, and to the greatest good of the Church of Christ.

And from the fact that the right use of forms of faith depends thus pre-eminently on the spirit in which they are regarded and employed, it of course follows that we cannot trust for the removal of the abuses connected with them to mere changes in their form, or in their terms. *Proper use of a creed depends rather on the wisdom of a Christian society than on provisions in regard to its form, or the mode of assent.* A good deal has been said of the desirableness of a brief creed, which would contain only such articles of belief as are absolutely essential. A good deal has also been said in favour of relaxing the formulas of assent and subscription. It would lead us into the discussion of subjects which are apart from the scope of this chapter, were we to enter fully into the consideration of these points; because they are points of detail, while we have endeavoured rather to treat the question of creeds on general grounds. This much, however, may be remarked that the provisions to which we have referred are not so certain to be effectual in securing religious tolerance as is sometimes imagined. The brevity of a form of belief, though it has manifest advantages, does not necessarily prevent its terms being made the subject of controversial warfare, and fierce party feeling. Thus the Nicene creed, notwithstanding its shortness, contains points which have given rise to conflicts of the most intense bitterness. In one case, the source of dispute was a single phrase of this creed;[1] in another, it was a difference represented by a single letter of a word.[2] And it is equally true that, though

[1] The phrase which expresses the procession of the Spirit from the Son,—"I believe in the Holy Ghost, who proceedeth from the Father *and the Son*." The question as to receiving or rejecting these words was one of the main circumstances which led to the rupture of the Greek and Latin Churches.

[2] The Church of the fourth century was convulsed during a long period by the controversy regarding the clause of the Nicene creed which represents Christ as "of one substance with the Father." The party opposed to this doctrine of the creed were willing to affirm that He was "of

the mode of expressing assent to a form of belief may be made general enough to suit the most comprehensive ideas, it is yet certain to be regarded by those who have no such sympathies in a narrower acceptation.[1] The truth is that intense religious feeling refuses to be controlled by minute phraseological considerations. When the spirit of bigotry is in full exercise, terms which are in themselves moderate are readily perverted to sustain the prepossessions of extreme partisanship. However important therefore the abbreviation of creeds, and the improvement of formulas of assent, it is not to such merely

like substance with the Father." The difference is represented in the original by one letter.

[1] This is shown, for instance, by the different interpretations put on the formula of assent to the Westminster Confession, commonly used by American Presbyterians. The Confession is assented to, according to this formula, as " containing the system of doctrine taught in the Holy Scriptures." Dr. Charles Hodge informs us that, while these words are wide enough to satisfy those like himself who refuse to be bound by every proposition of the Confession, they are at the same time interpreted by some much more widely than he approves, *and by others so strictly that their view of them could not be "practically carried out without dividing the Church into innumerable fragments!"* Appendix to Hodge's Commentary on Westminster Confession.

formal changes that we must mainly look for a comprehensive and reasonable view of a Church's belief. We must trust rather to the prevalence of wise and just sentiments. Those unwritten and undefinable elements of human opinion, which constitute the spirit of an age or a community, are the forces which operate most powerfully in determining the manner in which such a question will be treated. The fact, which we have endeavoured to illustrate, that the position given by Protestantism to creeds is a subsidiary one,—that they are confessedly imperfect and inferior to Scripture,—affords a sufficient reason for their being understood and applied with a wise allowance for the diversity of opinion which is an inevitable element of living religion.

CHAPTER VII.

THE PURITY OF THE CHURCH.

"Many in the communion of the Church are made better like Peter, many are tolerated like Judas, many are not known until the Lord shall come."—AUGUSTINE.

THE PURITY OF THE CHURCH.

THE corruptions and imperfections of the Christian Church have naturally awakened the regret of earnest Christians, and with it the desire to find some effectual remedy. From an early period in the history of Christianity attempts have been made to remove these disorders and to bring the Church into a condition of freedom from error and sin. The course by which the ardent maintainer of ecclesiastical purity has endeavoured to secure this object is the application of rigorous discipline. According to his view, it is owing to want of faithfulness in the administration of restrictive and corrective measures that a Christian communion is corrupt, and if due care is only taken to visit the offender against the laws of religion with censure, or with exclusion from the society of believers,

<small>The craving for a Pure Church.</small>

the end of securing a Pure Church will be attained. As early as the third century an important movement arose with the purpose of thus purifying the Church of Christ by the employment of methods of severe correction.[1] The party who assailed the existing state of discipline as insufficient and who were called "the Pure" on account of the strictness of the ecclesiastical standard which they advocated, went so far as to maintain that a Christian society which tolerates the existence of known offenders in its membership ceases thereby to be a true Church, and, moreover, that such offenders, having broken their baptismal vow, should not be readmitted to Christian communion. In the fourth and fifth centuries another important controversy occurred, notable partly for the share taken by Augustine in it, in which the exercise of discipline and the purity of the Church were again the points involved.[2] During subsequent ages in the history of the Church the views which were held thus early have been again and again revived. There have been frequent movements

[1] Known as the Schism of Novatianus. Neander, vol i. 336.

[2] Known as the Donatist Schism. Neander, vol. iii. 244.

in the direction of rigour of ecclesiastical discipline, as affording the only means of attaining the purity of the Church of Christ. Many of the divisions which have occurred in the Christian world have originated from this source. Earnest-minded persons, impressed with the vast difference between the state of the Christian Church, and the condition in which it should be, and fired with the longing to establish a faultless religious communion, have again and again sought, by the use of the most rigid measures, to create a scene of ecclesiastical perfection.

Now it has never been extensively questioned, and it does not seem as if it can on any reasonable ground be questioned, that the power of exercising discipline rightfully belongs to a Church. A religious society, like any other society, seems clearly entitled to possess the means of preserving itself from corruption and irregularity by the enforcement of order. The point, however, which involves matter of serious question is, to what extent this power, supposing it to be in itself lawful, should be carried? The opinion of the zealous upholder of an extremely strict regime is, that, the more exact the rule according to which

Question to be determined.

ecclesiastical order is maintained, and the more inexorably faults of life or belief are dealt with, the greater is the purity of a Church likely to be. But the testimony of facts, on the other hand, points to a very different conclusion. It shows, as we shall afterwards see, that measures of rigorous severity do not, in most instances, result in increased piety and virtue. There are, of course, exceptional cases—cases in which violation of the law of Christian well-doing is so gross and so conspicuous that nothing but extreme methods will suffice to vindicate the character of religion. But in relation to the failings and errors generally, which are to be found in a Christian communion, a system of stern repression leads to results the very opposite of those which it is designed to produce. So far from realizing his idea of ecclesiastical purity by rigour of discipline, the maintainer of such measures creates, rather than corrects, evil and error.

Scripture quoted to support extreme views of ecclesiastical purity. The quotations partial.

It is indeed true that those who argue in support of a system of extreme stringency appeal for their authority to certain passages of Scripture. They point to those many declarations of the sacred writers, which describe the Church of

Christ by such designations as "saints," the "sanctified in Christ Jesus," the "holy temple" of God, "the faithful brethren in Christ," the bride of Christ to be "presented to Himself without spot, or wrinkle, or any such thing";[1] and they urge that such descriptions are inconsistent with a state of things which allows the existence in the Church of acknowledged elements of evil. But, as often happens when passages of Scripture are produced in proof of a certain theory, there is in this instance a disregard of other, and very different, statements of Scripture. The representation which Christ repeatedly gives of the nature of His kingdom is, that in the present state of things, it is far from being absolutely pure. He likens it to the mingling of wheat and tares in the same field, and to the gathering together of good fish and bad in the same net, and He illustrates its character by the circumstance of foolish virgins being present in the marriage company along with the wise.[2] The New Testament Epistles also afford abundant evidence that the condition of the Christian Church, in times when it was recognized

---

[1] 1 Cor. i. 2 ; Eph. ii. 21 ; Col. i. 2 ; Eph. v. 27.
[2] Matt. xiii. 24-30 ; 47-50 ; xxv. 1-13.

by the Apostles themselves as the true communion of Christ, was very far from being exempt from corruption. There were many serious errors and many deviations from moral rectitude in the societies which enjoyed apostolic sanction and instruction.

<small>Confusion between the actual and the ideal states of the Church.</small>

The mistake committed by those who insist on applying to the present condition of the Church those descriptions of it as a pure and perfect communion, which are to be found in Scripture, is, that they fail to distinguish between its actual, and its ideal state. It is a feature of the New Testament,—as it necessarily is of all forms of truth which seek the elevation of human nature,—that it appeals to a standard, which is higher than what is realized in actual experience. Its mode of instruction proceeds on the principle that men are to be taught purity by conceptions of it more lofty than have yet been fulfilled in human life. It places before us, in short, an ideal to be aimed at, which is far above the point that the existing attainments of man have reached. And, as we have said, this is not a feature peculiar to the teachings of Christianity. All systems and modes of appeal, which address themselves to the elevation of man, make use of the same principle. They propose some ideal higher than has yet been grasped. The influence which they exercise depends on the measure of success with which they set before the minds of men conceptions of the true and good, that rise above the actual level of human attainment. The fact, therefore, that; while there are numerous statements in the New Testament, which declare the imperfect character of the Christian Church, and which refer to its corruptions and errors; there are also many representations of it in terms expressive of its holiness and superiority to the world; is but an instance of the mode of teaching that aims at exalting the thoughts and life by the exhibition of a perfect standard. It is in the same way that the Scriptures refer to the individual Christian character. They often describe it rather in its ideal completeness than in its actual condition. Thus the Christian is represented as being "dead to sin," as "having crucified the flesh with the affections and lusts," as "having put off the old man," as being "complete in Christ." This is language indicative more of the true and ultimate type of the Christian character than of what has been yet attained. It represents the nature of the new life in the light of its full development, and not in its defectiveness and sinfulness. And so, by means of a mode of instruction which gives prominence to the highest aspects of religion, the Scriptures furnish an incentive to spiritual effort, —they teach us, by the loftiness of the standard which they propose, that the end which we must seek gradually to reach is that of Christian perfection.

Effect of this confusion.

Overlooking the existence of this ideal element in the teaching of Scripture, the upholder of rigid ecclesiastical discipline commits the mistake of interpreting those passages which refer to the perfection of the Church as if they afford a rule that can be acted on in its existing state. He thus attempts to enforce a measure of purity, which it is impossible to realize. He takes the erroneous course which is represented in the Parable of the Wheat and Tares, when the servants of the householder are described as proposing to gather out the tares from amidst the wheat, and their master prohibits them, and says that both must grow together until the harvest. The ecclesiastical rigour that would create a pure communion by the enforcement of discipline is precisely analogous to the short-sighted suggestion of the servants in the parable. It seeks to root out the tares from amidst the wheat even now. It attempts to force upon the Church a condition of purity, which in present circumstances is impracticable. "Let both grow together until the harvest" is the general law of Christ in reference to His Church. Truth and falsehood, righteousness and sin, sincerity and hypocrisy must be allowed, in large measure, to exist in combination within the sphere of avowed Christianity; because any endeavour that can be made wholly to do away with this state of things at present is not only useless, but productive of evil. It is by the slow growth of good, and its gradual conquest of the opposite influences of sin; and not by the force of severity operating through outward measures; that we are to look for the final triumph of religion. While the mingling of error and sin with the purer elements of the Church does not satisfy the visionary aspirations of those who would put an end to ecclesiastical imperfections at once, it is really best that

The law of Christ.

such a state of things should in the meantime continue.

There are many considerations which justify the wisdom of the principle asserted by our Lord in relation to the purity of His Church; and which show that to attempt the eradication of the error and evil that exist in it, by means of rigorous measures, is at once vain and hurtful.

<small>Impossibility of separating between the good and the evil in the present state of things</small>

One main consideration is that which Christ Himself intimates in the Parable of the Wheat and Tares, when he represents the householder as prohibiting his servants from gathering out the tares from among the wheat, "lest, while they gathered up the tares, they should root up also the wheat with them." The application of this to a society of professing Christians is obvious. There are not the means of distinguishing character, in a religious communion, with such truth as to be able to bring external measures of purification to bear on it with anything like accuracy. In any case in which a stringent system of ecclesiastical discipline is imposed, the good are confounded with the evil. There are, as we have said, outstanding instances of wrong-doing which are unmistakeable; and which, when they bring injury on a religious body, and constitute a grave offence against its common sentiments, it may be necessary to visit with severity. Within the province of such flagrant transgressions the exercise of discipline may be far from unprofitable or needless. But, except in those cases in which evil and its injurious consequences stand so clearly out that to pass it over would be attended with results detrimental to a religious society, the exercise of discipline does more harm than good. Whenever it is attempted to apply corrective measures to an extent beyond this, the gravest possible mistakes necessarily follow. For human judgment can penetrate with certainty only a little way into the moral state of a community. It is unable to form anything like a true estimate of the minute circumstances and conditions that go to constitute the culpability or goodness of men. There are a thousand things lying beyond immediate observation, which materially affect the nature of actions; and which, were they known to us, would in many cases lead to a reversal of the opinion we entertain at a first view. It sometimes happens that the external demonstration of piety, which passes without question in a religious communion, proves to be insincere. There are not a few instances, on the other hand, in which the life that is marked by grave defects is also a life of real worth. The fault, which brings down on an offender a sentence of condemnation, would sometimes, if all the circumstances were known, be hardly regarded as a fault. In those who are so reserved and unpretending in reference to religion, that they are apt to be considered as outside the circle of the faithful, there is often more genuine religious earnestness than in the avowedly and conspicuously devout. There are thus endless and insuperable difficulties in the way of creating a pure state of the Church by means of rigorous discipline. Questions of human conduct are so complicated; and good and evil, truth and error, are united together in actual experience by such close and subtle relations; that it is altogether beyond the power of human discernment to distinguish truly in each case. The attempt to do so only leads to fatal confusion and mistake.

The freedom of the religious life requires And it is a not less valid objection to a system of ecclesiatical rigour that it is inconsistent with the liberty which properly belongs to the religious life. There cannot be freedom in the religious sphere, any more than in other provinces of human action, unless a large toleration is allowed to evil and error. The latitude which, Christ declared, must be permitted in the Church, "Let the wheat and the tares grow together until the harvest," is the necessary condition of spiritual freedom. Let us suppose that, by the adoption of extremely exacting terms of communion, and by a stern discipline, an exclusion of certain elements of evil from a Christian society is effected, what is the result? While a measure of purity —at least, of an outward kind—is thus produced, it is the consequence of a system of restraint. It has not arisen from voluntary conviction. It is not the growth of living and spontaneous feeling. The external amendment, which is thus introduced into a religious communion, is due simply to the action of restrictive force. And therefore it is not deeply rooted. It has no thoroughness, or permanence. It is only when ample liberty is allowed to the exercise of the moral and spiritual powers, and when the conscience and judgment are left to operate without

that there must be toleration of evil.

the influence of unnecessary restriction, that true religious life can exist and prosper. Hence the condition of the Christian Church, in which a large tolerance is given to human conduct, is the only one that is suited to the development of religion in its true vigour and fulness. A Christian society that imposes on its members a system of stringent requirement, and that follows them into their actions with a rigid control, if it produces religious purity of a kind, produces an unhealthy type of it. The piety which it nourishes is the result of constraint. It is, on the other hand, when a Church trusts, not to restrictions from without, but to the power of truth and the effect of spiritual influences, that it really most promotes the interests of purity; just because it recognizes, in this case, the individual freedom, which is involved in all sound religious life.

Testimony of history. The facts of Christian history afford abundant evidence of the truth of this statement. In those instances, in which extreme strictness has been associated with religion, it has not, as a rule, produced the desired effects. Thus, in the period when Puritan austerity was in the ascendant, and religion was surrounded with the restraints of a severe discipline, the result was not favourable to the prevalence of virtue. There is strong evidence that the opposite was the case.[1] Never probably was ecclesiastical discipline carried out with more systematic stringency than by the Presbyterians of a former age. It was applied by them with a faithfulness that spared no one, whatever his circumstances or his rank. The regulation of domestic devotion, attendance at public worship, the observance of the Sabbath, the actions of daily life, and the very words that were spoken, were treated as proper subjects for ecclesiastical censorship. Offences, not only against the moral law, but against religious usages, were visited with a severity which might well have remedied the errors and evils of human nature, had this been the true method of dealing with them.

---

[1] The austere discipline of Puritanism had never probably a fairer field for the exhibition of its results than in New England. Cotton Mather's History, though written in the spirit of an admirer, gives a very dark picture of the crimes which stained society in New England under this ecclesiastical rule. The incidents which he relates under the head of Remarkable Judgments of God, and Dying Speeches of Criminals are of the most heinous description. Magnalia Christi Americana, or the Ecclesiastical History of New England, 1620—98.

The actual result, however, was very different. Instead of this period in ecclesiastical history having been distinguished by extraordinary virtue, its rigorous asterity seems to have had precisely the contrary effect.[1]

Natural results of over-strictness. Such facts bear out the remarks we have made. They are an illustration of the truth which we have affirmed, that a religious system which denies freedom to human feeling and action, and which trusts to mere restraint, is not true or healthy, and therefore must lead to evil consequences. When the natural dispositions of men are checked by stringent measures, they assert for themselves a liberty all the worse and more dangerous that they are sternly repressed. Desires and tendencies, which are prevented from having reasonable indulgence, are sure to find other outlets for themselves. And especially does this mischievous result of over-strictness arise in connection with the antagonism of religious persons to the enjoyments of life. This has always

[1] Chambers, in his Domestic Annals of Scotland, gives an unfavourable account of the state of morals there during the period of Presbyterian rigour; and, as the statements are derived from a variety of contemporary sources, there can be little doubt of their substantial accuracy. Vol. i., 333; ii., 161, 197, &c.

been one of the characteristics of excessive ecclesiastical rigour. The element of human pleasure, even though harmless, has been regarded as incompatible with religion; and piety has been supposed to be consistent only with moroseness and gloom. So it was according to Puritan ideas. So it was in the rigorous age of Presbyterianism, to which we have alluded. The joys of the world were frowned upon as being irreconcilable with Christian earnestness; and to be demure and precise was considered as alone fulfilling the true idea of the religious character. Now, there is involved in this view a source of inevitable evil. The craving for enjoyment is a feeling so natural and powerful, that it is certain to be indulged in some form. If it is interdicted in those directions in which its exercise is harmless, or in which there is least liability for it to become a cause of evil, it assumes depraved modes of development. The undisguised and healthful indulgence of the desire for pleasure is a safeguard in some measure of the interests of virtue. It provides innocent gratification for a disposition inherent in our nature. The very absence of constraint, which the maintainer of austere notions of religion disapproves in the more cheerful forms of human enjoyment, is, in point of fact, what may with justice be urged, from a moral point of view, in their favour: for it is not in such cheerful relaxations from the labour and anxieties of life that men incur the risk of sinning, so much as in those modes of self-indulgence that wear the mask of gravity and strictness. But this the upholder of an austere precision overlooks. He wishes to suppress the brighter and opener manifestations of human enjoyment, and imagines that by making life dull and decorous he brings it into accordance with piety; forgetting, all the while, that the effect of denying to natural feeling its reasonable exercise is to drive men to wrong courses, that, with the prohibition of such enjoyment as has a recognized place in social life, a stimulus is given to other and lower pleasures.

Hence, then, the entire failure of those attempts which have been made to render the Church of Christ pure by the application of measures of extreme rigour. They involve the error of endeavouring to effect by means of restraint what can only be accomplished by the more gradual influences of truth and love. Human nature, when subjected to over-restriction, rebels against it, and is made worse instead of better.

And, while the endeavour to force an impossible standard of purity on the Church is thus apt to lead to a reaction, and to produce vice rather than to prevent it; it has also results not less injurious in the tone of religious feeling which it implies and fosters. This is described with graphic force by one of the Reformers, who says, "We must not require that the Church, while in this world, should be free from every wrinkle and stain; or forthwith pronounce unworthy of such a title every society in which everything is not as we would wish it. For it is a dangerous temptation to think that there is no Church at all where perfect purity is not seen. For the man that is prepossessed with this notion must necessarily in the end withdraw from all others, and look upon himself as the only saint in the world, or set up a peculiar sect in company with a few hypocrites."[1] The attempt, in other words, to create an absolutely pure Church has the effect of producing a spirit of religious pride and hypocrisy; because it is an essentially vain and delusive idea. The

[1] Calvin's Commentary on 1 Corinthians.

worst effect of visionary theories is not their failure, but the false state of feeling to which they lead. When men come to believe in things which are no better than idle dreams, and to make these the object of their efforts, the result is that they are brought under the influence of fictitious sentiments. They live in an unreal world; and thus their whole nature acquires a character of unreality. Therefore it is that those, who set themselves to form a religious communion which is to be superior to the errors and imperfections of ordinary humanity, naturally fall under the power of a delusive self-exaltation and hypocrisy. The view which they try to work out is untrue, and they become themselves infected with its untruth. When we endeavour to carry out a standard of sanctity in the actual conditions of life, which these conditions render utterly impossible, the certain consequence is spiritual deterioration. We can persuade ourselves that such a high standard is attained only by self-deception. Hence the truth of Calvin's graphic description, when he represents the man, with an extravagant idea of the purity which should be found in the Church, arriving at last at a state of solitary self-glorification, or "setting up a peculiar sect in company with a few hypocrites." Such instances have been abundantly common in Christian history—instances in which the separatist, filled with the chimerical fancy of establishing a perfect Church of Christ on earth, only succeeds in fostering delusion and pretence.

And not only does the attempt to bring about a condition of absolute purity in the Church lead to the existence of hypocrisy by the unreal standard of human conduct which it sets up, but it also produces the same effect in another way. For the enforcement of over-rigid ideas of religion, with which an extravagant view of ecclesiastical sanctity is necessarily accompanied, always produces falseness of feeling and life. When, under the profession of religious strictness, men oppose and despise those usages and enjoyments which are in themselves harmless, there may be the most perfect sincerity in many instances, but in many other cases it is far otherwise. Excessive rigour has a natural kinship to hypocrisy. The minute precision, which assigns importance to the least form; the severity of manner, which is a perpetual condemnation of

Connection of excessive rigour with hypocrisy.

human pleasure; and the stringency, which lets no fault of others, however trifling, escape its reproach; afford a congenial style of character for the dissembler to cultivate. While he thus appears to be zealous for religion, it is not a zeal which costs him the sacrifice of any vice, or the performance of any real virtue. The austerity he manifests is quite reconcilable with the indulgence of the worst spiritual faults, such as malice and pride; while it is also compatible with the secret practice of immorality. Indeed, the very scrupulousness which is characteristic of a system of excessive rigour is itself peculiarly fatal to moral purity and truth; for the scruples of the rigorist are commonly about what is of least importance. It is in reference to the "mint, and anise, and cummin," that he is particular; while the great matters of the law are overlooked by him. Little points and trifling distinctions usurp the attention that should be bestowed on the performance of the essential obligations of religion. And thus the application of a too rigid idea to the state of the Christian Church ends in its corruption and decay. The effort to impose on it conditions of purity which are impracticable leads to its sinking into impurity. It becomes a scene, not of moral perfection, but of moral decadence. So it was in the history of the Puritans, for example. It is thus that the historian describes the ultimate stage in the course of events, which marked the downfall of that system of religious rigour. " What were then considered as the signs of real godliness : the sad-coloured dress, the sour look, the straight hair, the speech interspersed with quaint texts, the Sunday gloomy as a Pharisaical Sabbath, were easily imitated by men to whom all religions were the same. The sincere Puritans soon found themselves lost in a multitude, not merely of men of the world, but of the very worst sort of men of the world. For the most notorious libertine, who had fought under the royal standard, might justly be thought virtuous compared with some of those who, while they talked about sweet experiences and comfortable scriptures, lived in the constant practice of fraud, rapacity, and secret debauchery. The people, with a rashness which we may justly lament, but at which we cannot wonder, formed their estimate of the whole body from these hypocrites. The

It leads to moral deterioration. Illustrated by the case of the Puritans.

theology, the manners, the dialect of the Puritans were thus associated in the public mind with the darkest and meanest vices. A general outcry against Puritanism rose from every corner of the kingdom, and was often swollen by the voices of those very dissemblers, whose villainy had brought disgrace on the Puritan name." [1]

<small>Survey of previous arguments.</small>

It thus appears from our consideration of this subject that, though it is so often thought that the Church of Christ can be brought into a state of purity by means of disciplinary measures, such a view is far from being correct. The divine wisdom of the principle laid down by Christ, " Let the wheat and the tares grow together until the harvest," has been fully proved by the facts of Christian history. The experiments which have been made in the direction of producing a faultless condition of the Church have only resulted in manifesting the truth of the rule implied in Christ's words. Instead of greater purity arising from those endeavours which have been made to extirpate error and sin from the communion of Christians, their effect has been

---

[1] Lord Macaulay's History of England, chap. ii.

favourable in many instances to hypocrisy and moral declension.

The true use of discipline, on the other hand, consists, we have endeavoured to show, in its limitation to those instances in which evil is so flagrant, and its bad consequences so manifest, that to pass it over without correction would endanger the order of a Christian communion. But to do more than this is, we have argued, certain to result in harm. To presume to sit in judgment on the motives and the spiritual state of men, and to drag into the light men's private actions, in place of being conducive to ecclesiastical purity, is entirely adverse to it. Unless liberty is allowed for the exercise of the conscience, and for the operation of a sense of personal responsibility, there cannot, we have maintained, be healthy spiritual life in a Church.

And, while the teaching of Christ sustains this view, it is not less plainly the view on which the Apostles acted. The instance which chiefly exemplifies the apostolic judgment on the subject is that of the Corinthian Church. Although that community of believers had become infected with evils of a very serious kind; although the

Apostolic view of the subject.

prevalence of party strife, the introduction of irregularities into the mode of celebrating the Lord's Supper, and certain abuses which had come to be common in connection with the exercise of spiritual gifts, were blots on its Christian character; St. Paul does not hesitate to apply to it the epithet, "Church of God."[1] Nay, he describes it as consisting of "them that are sanctified in Christ Jesus, called to be saints."[2] It is plain, therefore, that he was very far from entertaining the visionary idea of the Church of Christ, which regards it as a society exempt from the common defects of human nature. This, however, is not all that the example of St. Paul in the case of the Corinthian Church illustrates in reference to the subject of ecclesiastical purity. For there was in the Christian community at Corinth a case which demanded, according to the Apostle's view, the exercise of decisive discipline; and he consequently directed that the offender should be excluded from the communion of the Church. But the case which he thus dealt with was of the most heinous character; it was so peculiarly flagrant as to be unknown, he tells us,

[1] 1 Cor. i. 2.   [2] Id.

"even among the Gentiles."[1] And, when the culprit afterwards evinced a penitent spirit, the Apostle was not less anxious for his restoration than he had previously been decided on the necessity of his exclusion.[2]

We have thus, in St. Paul's treatment of the circumstances of the Corinthian Church, a clear illustration of the position he assumed in reference to the general subject of the purity of the Church, and also of his judgment as to the application of discipline. In relation to the first point, his attitude is that of one who was ready to recognize in an exceedingly imperfect communion, a communion marred by many grave faults, a "Church of God," a society of the "sanctified in Christ Jesus." In relation to the second, he plainly shows that he considered that the administration of measures of severity should be reserved to such cases as are exceptional in their heinousness and notoriety.

Unhappily the wisdom which characterizes the teaching of the New Testament in this respect has, as we have seen, largely failed to distinguish the ecclesiastical history of succeeding ages. Never- *[Undue stringency protested against even when it was in the ascendant.]*

[1] 1 Cor. v. 1.   [2] 2 Cor. ii. 6-8.

theless, even in periods when a mistaken rigour was much more the rule than it has ever been in modern times, there were not wanting those who gave utterance to sentiments adverse to the attempt to keep men right by a stern discipline, and who advocated the use of other methods as being alone in accordance with the Gospel. Thus, shortly after the Reformation, there was one whose testimony was forcibly raised against the undue stringency which he believed the Reformed Church was using in reference to the conditions of communion. His theory of discipline, indeed, is untenable, and is now hardly, if at all, maintained; while many of the arguments which he adduced in its support will not bear examination.[1] He gave expression, at the

---

[1] An Examination of that Most Grave Question whether Excommunication, or the Debarring from the Sacraments of Professing Christians because of their Sins, be a Divine Ordinance or a Human Invention, by the renowned Thomas Erastus, Doctor of Medicine. 1659. Erastus, whose work on excommunication is thus described in the title of the old English translation of the above date, flourished a century previously, 1524-1583. He denied that the Church had any right to excommunicate offenders, and maintained that, where offences are committed by members of the Church, they fall to be punished by the civil power. Because he advocated the intervention of the civil magistrate

same time, to many things which are just and striking, on the subject of endeavouring to keep the Church of Christ pure by extreme strictness. He refers thus to Christ's own example as being against the limitation of the privileges of a Church to a select circle—"Christ Himself entered always into the same temple with Pharisees, with Sadducees, with publicans and all others, bad and good alike; He assisted at the same sacrifices with them; He used the same sacraments of which the whole Jewish community partook; and also He

to deal with ecclesiastical offences, his name has been handed down in the sinister epithets "Erastian" and "Erastianism." Though his theory is indefensible, he deserves to be remembered in a very different way. The extracts from his Theses given above show him to have been not less humane in his views of discipline than he was, by the admission of some of his distinguished contemporaries, learned and upright. So far from desiring to reduce the Church into bondage to the civil power, it is evident from his Theses that he wished, by bringing in the civil power, to deliver members of the Church from ecclesiastical tyranny. He says that the Reformed clergy of his own times were going to prove as despotic as the Pope. (Thesis 72.) He plainly thought that the civil magistrate would be a more merciful administrator of punishment than the clergy. The above extracts are from the Theses of Erastus, translated from the Latin by Dr. Robert Lee, Edinburgh.

received from John the Baptist the same baptism which was administered to all those nefarious characters mentioned in the Gospel history. For the same reason Christ did not hinder Judas who betrayed Him from eating the last paschal lamb, but he sat down with the other eleven disciples."[1] In answer to the argument that an offender should be prevented from receiving the sacraments on the ground that he may return to his sinful life, he says—"Whether such a man shall persevere in his holy resolution, and how long, God knows. It is ours always to hope the best regarding all men, even though we should be often deceived, and also from the heart to beseech God to establish both them and ourselves in what is good."[2] He makes the observation—"If men are deprived of the invitation to the sacraments, they will never grow better, but always worse."[3] In reference to the officebearers of a Church taking on them the function of separating the good from the bad, he says—"The Apostle Paul, speaking of celebrating the communion, does not appoint that we should examine one another, and ascertain whether some one may not be there who might defile us, but

[1] Theses of Erastus, 27, 28.   [2] Id. 37.   [3] Id. 66.

this is his command, 'Let every man examine, not others, but himself.'"[1] "Who but God," he further remarks, "is the judge of men's hearts? It may happen that some spark may be kindled by the public preaching, which it may be not at all useless, but rather most beneficial, to cherish by every means not inconsistent with piety. And tell me, I pray, how can it be otherwise than absurd, and therefore impious, to debar from a solemn thanksgiving and commemoration of the death of the Lord a person who declares that he feels his heart prompts him so to do?—that he desires with the Church to celebrate that death and to be a member of the Church, and, finally, that he wishes to testify that he disapproves his past life."[2]

The spirit expressed in these statements represents with far greater truth the proper attitude of Christianity with reference to human error and sinfulness than does the opinion that they are to be remedied by the enforcement of stringent measures. While corrective means are not without their use in relation to the evil that exists in the Church, the most powerful agency

The ministry of Christ a pattern to the Church.

[1] Theses of Erastus, 67. [2] Id. 75.

for its removal is only to be found in far other influences—in the power of Christian teaching, and in the realization of Christ's sacrifice and example. The ministry of our Lord Himself exhibits the power which belongs to the mode of treating human nature that is based on sympathy and mercy. His entire work of teaching, and awakening, and converting proceeded upon the fact that these ends are to be accomplished mainly by the use of persuasion, and by the manifestation of love. His power in raising the fallen depended on this method of dealing with man. He restored the sinful to new hope and life by receiving them freely to His presence and His friendship. He strengthened those who were deficient in moral courage, and lacking in faithfulness, by the pity He showed to them in their infirmities. Those whom Christ addressed in terms of severe rebuke, and whom He condemned with unsparing plainness, were such as judged with self-righteous arrogance regarding others, and who maintained an appearance of strictness, which their lives belied. He denounced their spirit and life as being false and bad. But, on the other hand, the publicans and sinners rejoiced in His word. It is in following the example of Christ that the Church is alone likely to fulfil its true mission to the world,—in seeking to reclaim the offender, and to build up the faithful, by methods of forbearance and sympathy, rather than of rigour.

CHAPTER VIII.

CONCLUSION.

"There is nothing which is not some way excelled even by that which it doth excel."—HOOKER.

CONCLUSION.

We propose to state in this concluding chapter some general results to which the preceding discussions lead.

<small>*Ecclesiastical subjects often treated too theoretically.*</small>

Prominent among the features which they illustrate is the fact referred to in the Preface, that ecclesiastical subjects have been dealt with, to a large extent, on grounds of mere theory, instead of being judged of in accordance with human nature and human experience. This is an error not infrequently committed also in reference to the ordinary problems of social life. Ideas, imposing and attractive, but inconsistent with the actual conditions of the world, are often propounded for the removal of the evils of society, and the adjustment of its affairs. It is always found, however, that when these ideas are translated from the region of the abstract into the actual experience of life, they do not at all accomplish what was expected from them—that, in many instances, they are productive of serious evil. The reason is, that the actual conditions of existence are so different from what any merely theoretic system can provide for, that human concerns do not admit of being regulated in this way. They require, on the contrary, to be treated mainly by practical methods. Considerations of expediency, and a careful regard to varying circumstances, are the elements which must chiefly be applied to the determination of the questions involved in the common affairs of the world.

Now, while the mistake of applying merely theoretic views to the problems of human conduct is one that has been common in the sphere of ordinary social life, and has there led to not a few evils, it is a mistake which has been specially prevalent in regard to church questions. The ecclesiastic very often proclaims a certain idea as being alone true, and demands that that shall be adopted universally. Whether his idea is wisely adapted to existing necessities, whether it can be carried out with the best results, whether, indeed,

Conclusion. 273

it can practically be carried out at all, are considerations which are apt to be lost sight of. He maintains his ecclesiastical notions at all hazards. He sees nothing outside them that will be successful in fulfilling the divine will. His view is, not that ecclesiastical subjects are to be regarded in the light of their suitableness to the spiritual need of particular men, or of a particular time; nor yet that the chief thing is that a Church should hold and teach the truth; but that his own system should be upheld. He is not prepared to accommodate matters of polity to the various circumstances and desires of men, but expects that men will comply with what he regards as the only tenable form of polity.

This tendency to carry merely abstract ideas into the consideration of matters relating to the Church, instead of being guided by a regard to the facts of actual experience, is exemplified in much of the ecclesiastical opinion which has been touched upon in the preceding pages; and the evil consequences arising from it are also illustrated by many of the facts which have been stated. Thus we have seen that, by the adoption of a theory of purity in relation to the Christian

This tendency to merely theoretic ideas illustrated by opinions regarding the purity of the Church.

S

Church, without due consideration of the existing condition of human nature, many and serious abuses have been created. Nothing, it is true, can present a more inviting subject of speculation to the religious mind than to picture to itself the Church of Christ as a perfectly holy communion—a communion free from error, and from moral stain. But it is theory, not fact; it is the ideal, not the actual, condition of the Church. And, therefore, when, as has often been done, this abstract conception of the Church has been attempted to be realized in its present state, the result has been to lead to mistakes and evils of the most serious kind.

Also by the view often held in regard to the unity of the Church.

In connection also with another subject which we have discussed—the unity of the Christian Church—there is a not less forcible example of an idea being prevalently accepted, which is entirely without foundation in human experience. For the view of Christian unity which is so commonly held—that all believers in Christ should hold precisely the same belief, and observe the same forms of worship, and belong to the same external religious society, and that any exception to uniformity in these respects is due to their sinfulness—is a view which proceeds on an absolute disregard of the acknowledged facts of our nature. In no sphere of thought and life, in which men act freely, was there ever such unity. The only oneness which is expected in national existence, and in the relations of the world at large, is such as is attended with many and great diversities. The truth is recognized in political society, and in the everyday concerns of life, that differences of sentiment and action must be allowed for as a necessary condition of human fellowship. Nay, it is fully admitted, in reference to the ordinary social relations of the world, that those diversities of opinion and temperament which lead men to take different sides are, upon the whole, a source of good—that they tend to maintain the interests of truth by preventing narrow and partial conclusions. And yet, in spite of this indubitable testimony of facts, the idea is still very extensively held that there ought to be no differences of view among Christians; that, to use a familiar expression, they should "see eye to eye"; and that the bond which should connect them ought to be that of absolute identity of faith and absolute sameness of polity and form. Now, what are the necessary consequences of attempting to carry out a notion of religious unity so opposed to the facts of human nature? Like all endeavours to bring men into conformity with a visionary standard, it has led to great evil. The dogma of an absolute literal unity of the Church, is what has constituted the animating principle of intolerance in all its various forms. It is in pursuance of this belief that forcible efforts have been resorted to to suppress variations of religious opinion. It is this view which lies at the root of ecclesiastical bigotry and exclusiveness. Let it be admitted that the bond which unites men in a common Christianity is, like that which connects them in other relations, one which allows freedom for the existence of varieties of thought and form, and a principle is then recognized which renders a wide religious accord practicable. But, on the other hand, the idea of Christian unity which regards it as equivalent to a state of absolute external agreement is fraught with all the evils of endless intolerance and contention.

Further illustrated by the lofty ecclesiasti- Nor is there a less striking proof of the evils of a merely theoretic view of ecclesiastical subjects in those claims to exclusive divine right which, as we have seen, have been so often and so zealously advanced by contending ecclesiastical parties. Nothing could show more forcibly the extent to which men will go in imagining that they have discovered conclusive evidence for what is only a visionary prepossession than do the claims which have thus been urged in support of the various modes of church government. What a humorous writer has said in regard to preaching—that, when the preacher has made up his mind what to say, any text will serve his purpose—may with truth be applied to the kind of evidence which is apt to satisfy men who have made up their minds to believe in the sole divine authority of a certain church-system. We have pointed out, in our remarks on the relation of Scripture to ecclesiastical subjects, that the most extraordinary interpretations of the Sacred Volume have been resorted to by those who have tried to deduce from its pages an express sanction for their respective forms of ecclesiastical polity. The result has been that Presbyterianism has been traced back to the giving of the law from Mount Sinai, while it has been made out that Episcopacy dates from the age of

cal claims of church parties.

Adam. The truth is that a certain theory of church government was, first of all, assumed as true by those who made such discoveries in Scripture, and texts were afterwards found which appeared to them to sustain it. And the view of those who advocate lofty ecclesiastical claims on the ground, not of alleged warrant for their particular form of polity in Scripture, but of alleged unbroken succession in the transmission of orders from the Apostles, really exemplifies, it appears to us, the same process of first embracing a theory, and then adopting a certain line of proof in support of it. For it is difficult to believe that any one would advance such a chimerical argument in favour of the divine right of a Church as the assertion of the extremely doubtful doctrine of the derivation of its orders from the Apostles; just as it is difficult to believe that any one would call in the history of the Adamic age and the law of Moses as evidence to the same effect; were there not a preconceived opinion to maintain.[1]

[1] " What is the degree of satisfactory assurance afforded to scrupulous consciences by the doctrine of apostolic succession ? If a man consider it as highly probable that the particular minister at whose hands he receives the

And, while the foundation on which the extravagant claims of competing church-systems are based is of such a theoretic character, the aspirations which are entertained by those who advocate them are not less so. It is not uncommon to find the champion of an ecclesiastical

> sacred ordinances is really apostolically descended, this is the very utmost point to which he can attain, and the more he reflects and enquires the more cause for hesitation he will find. There is not a minister in all Christendom who is able to trace up with any approach to certainty his own spiritual pedigree.... Let anyone proceed on the hypothesis that there are, suppose, but a hundred links connecting any particular minister with the Apostles, and let him suppose that not above half of this number pass through such periods as admit of any possible irregularity, and then placing at the lowest estimate the probability of defectiveness in respect of each of the remaining fifty, taken separately, let him consider what amount of probability will result from the multiplying of the whole together. The ultimate consequence must be that any one who sincerely believes that his claim to the benefits of the Gospel covenant depends on his own minister's claim to the supposed sacramental virtue of true ordination, and this again on perfect apostolical succession, must be involved, in proportion as he reads, and enquires, and reflects, and reasons on the subject, in the most distressing doubt and perplexity. It is no wonder that the advocates of this theory studiously disparage reasoning, deprecate all exercise of the mind in reflection, and decry appeals to evidence." Archbishop Whately's Kingdom of Christ, p. 175.

Theoretic character of ecclesiastical views further shown by the visionary aspirations connected with them.

party urging its exclusive right to be considered as the Church of Christ, and proclaiming what amounts to an assertion of its being the sole refuge and home of such light and grace as exist in this world. But what, according to this view, is to become of the rest of mankind? How, in this case, are the blessings of Christianity to be extended to the human race in general? The conclusion obviously is, that all Christian people who are of a different way of thinking from those who form the ecclesiastical party in question are to surrender their own views and become converts to the beliefs and religious forms of this particular body. No idea could well be more absurdly visionary. It involves oblivion of all the real conditions with which the Church of Christ has to deal—oblivion of the diversified needs of the world, and of the variety which must of necessity characterize the development of living religion. So that, though a Christian society may be wisely constituted and traditionally venerable, though it may be able justly to claim for itself a great deal that entitles it to honour, there can be no greater mistake than for it to claim that men must come within its fold if they would have the blessings of salvation. It is, in point of fact, but another instance of the extent to which men are apt to be misled by mere dreams. It contemplates an event which will never happen. Human nature is too diversely constituted ever to submit to the demand that it shall lay aside its individual beliefs, and accept the alleged authority of any one religious body.

From the instances which we have thus stated it is apparent that purely theoretical ideas have largely influenced the treatment of church-questions. What, on the other hand, has been mainly urged in the preceding discussions on subjects relating to the Church is the adoption of different ground. The principle which it has been sought to apply is that ecclesiastical matters should be regarded rather from the side of human feeling and human wants. It seems to be quite as great a mistake, and to be productive of quite as mischievous consequences, to endeavour to adjust the problems of the Church by merely abstract notions as it is to settle the affairs of human life in general by the same means. The true ground of judgment in regard to the former, as in regard to the latter, appears to be the consideration of what is

The true standard by which ecclesiastical matters should be estimated that of facts and experience.

most for the promotion of the good of men. Whether a church system is Episcopal, or Presbyterian, or Independent, or of some other type, is altogether a smaller question than whether, in the circumstances, it is well suited to advance the great ends of religion. What our Lord said of the Sabbath to those who advocated an impossible idea of Sabbath-keeping may with truth be applied to the Church—ecclesiastical institutions were made for man, and not man for them. And, therefore, the chief thing is, are they practically wise and good? do they efficiently fulfil their object in making men better? That appears to be a matter of infinitely more concern than what the particular mode of church government or system of ritual may be.

<small>Objection stated to this view.</small> By those who regard ecclesiastical subjects from the other point of view this principle of dealing with them has been objected to on the ground that it advocates, or at least encourages, a feeling of indifference with respect to them. That, however, is not by any means a just opinion. It does not follow, because a man has no faith in the lofty assertions which are made by the ecclesiastical partisan in behalf of his Church, that he has there-

fore no decided convictions of his own on the subject. He may believe that it is not an essential point what mode of church-order men embrace; and yet, at the same time, he may entertain an unequivocal preference for one ecclesiastical system rather than others. The exercise of special predilections in this respect is a different thing from bigotry. And it seems unquestionable that those feelings of partiality which men have for the Christian communion to which they belong, and for the forms of worship which they observe, are, within reasonable limits, beneficial. While, to a certain extent, they circumscribe Christian action, they give to it greater practical effect. The energies of human nature are never so strongly developed as when they are exercised within definite lines. And hence we think it may be truly held that those sectional distinctions which exist in the ecclesiastical world, although they have been accompanied with many evils, represent also an element of good. The individuality which is given to religious thought and effort by their limitation to certain channels is a source of benefit. Were the characteristic features which distinguish one section of Christians from another to be obliterated, the effect would not be to enrich religion as a whole, but to make it poorer. Therefore we are very far from arguing in support of an indifferentism that would decry all predilections in favour of one ecclesiastical form or other. We argue only against the error of erecting one's own partialities into a law for everyone.

<small>No perfection in any one ecclesiastical system.</small>

And it should also be remembered that not only is the individuality which is given to religion by the existence of the distinctive forms of Christian life and thought an important good, but the very maintenance of truth is dependent on spiritual contrasts. It is not in any one type of opinion that the fulness of truth exists. It is rather in the blending of different, and even opposing, modes of thought. The profound observation of Hooker, which we have prefixed to this chapter, that "there is nothing which is not some way excelled even by that which it doth excel," expresses the principle by which alone we can attain to just conceptions of truth. There is no perfection of excellence in any system. If one system has its special merits as compared with another, it has also its defects. Truth and wisdom are not monopolized by any party. The bearing of this fact ecclesiastically is evident. It points to the existence of diversities of ecclesiastical type as having its use in leading to right opinion; inasmuch as it serves to bring into view those opposing elements of thought which are necessary to sound ideas. There is nothing more common than for an ecclesiastical society to be extolled by its partisans as combining in itself every imaginable excellence. They would have us believe that its efficiency is complete. But the truth is, that the very qualities which render an institution effective for certain ends are often its greatest danger; because they are liable to be carried to an excess, that makes them a source of evil. Thus take as an illustration the case of government by prelacy, as compared with that of those churches in which government is vested more or less in the people. There can be no doubt that, in the former instance, grave difficulties and disadvantages are avoided by the governing power not being in the hands of the many; but, at the same time, history conclusively proves that this, which is the very strength of the system, is also a source of most serious peril; for it is apt to lead, by an undue separation of the clergy from the people, to sacerdotalism. On the other hand, the admission of the popular element to the control of ecclesiastical affairs, while it removes in a great degree the risk of superstitious views of the clerical order and their functions, is not free from dangers of its own; it is liable to be attended at times by the fanaticism, which readily arises where the multitude have power. So it is that any system of church-polity, however great its merits, has its special elements of imperfection. The principles which it embodies easily admit of being developed so extravagantly as to lead to false results. And it is to the influence of contrasting views — to the counterbalance of opinion produced by various and opposing ideas—that we have, in great measure, to look for the correction of this tendency to extremes.

Hence we have endeavoured to point out, in treating of the subject of the unity of the Church, that the existence of a diversity of ecclesiastical bodies cannot justly be regarded as by any means the unmitigated evil that many esteem it; and that the fusion of all the various sections of Christians into one communion would not, even if practicable, be necessarily the blessing which it is so often supposed to be. In reference to religion, as in reference to all subjects, divergence of sentiment is a condition of living thought. The division of men into parties, with contrary views of things, is not only universal in regard to what awakens profound interest, but it is also a source of ultimate advantage to the cause of truth.

But this line of remark necessarily leads further. If diversity of opinion is thus inevitable as a condition of religious life, a Church must lay its account with this fact, if it would occupy a position of stability, and of wide usefulness. It is the quaint saying of an English bishop of former days that, if a Church be set on too narrow a basis, it will stand only as a boy's top stands when set on its sharp point—that is, so long as it is kept up by violent effort; but, on the other hand, if resting on a broad basis, it will stand of itself.[1] There is much

A Church should be comprehensive of differences of thought.

---

[1] Wilkins, Bishop of Chester, who was well known in the seventeenth century, on account not only of his talents and learning, but also his advocacy of liberal church views.

truth in this homely aphorism. Small and sectarian views are not lastingly strong. They owe their power to the zeal of the few, or to the peculiar circumstances of the time. They do not appeal to those general principles which are the permanent convictions of the human mind. And therefore a system which is founded on narrow ideas requires, while it exists, the application of continual exertion to sustain it; and eventually it must either essentially change, or perish. It is needful, then, that a Church should be comprehensive of varieties of thought, if it is to hold a place of wide and lasting religious influence. We fully admit, indeed, the necessity to an ecclesiastical body, as to any other society, of such disciplinary power as will enable it to protect itself from disorder. We admit that the exercise of such power may become absolutely necessary in regard to matters of opinion—that the danger to the well-being, and even the existence, of a Church, arising from unwarranted doctrines, may be so great as to require the employment of the authority possessed by it for its own conservation. But we have tried to show, in a previous chapter, that the Protestant view of creeds is not consistent with the despotic stringency that will allow no difference of religious sentiment. The creeds of Protestantism expressly disclaim all title to be regarded as perfect or infallible, and they refer to the Scriptures as the sole standard of belief. A priesthood which lays claim to infallibility holds its articles of faith to be, in every statement and syllable, absolutely true and divine. A religious society which discards all pretensions to the infallible accuracy of its articles, and avows their subordinateness to Scripture, occupies a different position. The logical conclusion from its position is, that it cannot consistently demand that the agreement of its members shall be such as to supersede all freedom, and therefore all diversity of judgment. And thus, while the right of a Church to preserve itself from disorder seems unquestionable, it seems equally true and equally important—judging from the Protestant point of view—that there should be no such "lordship over faith"[1] as seeks to suppress all deviations from an absolutely rigid standard. It is in maintaining liberty along with order that the

[1] 2 Cor. i. 24, Rev. Version.

strength of a Church, as of any other social body, must in a great degree consist. The ecclesiastical society may therefore be expected to be the strongest and most enduring which embodies this principle—which makes a wise allowance for difference of views.

A Church should also allow variety of form. And the same thing holds in reference to matters of polity and form as we have now remarked in regard to questions of belief. A Church must have greater efficiency and influence for good, when it makes its religious forms comprehensive and varied enough to adapt them to the manifoldness of Christian wants, than when it is guided by one-sided traditions in this respect. To attempt to confine Christian faith and devotion within the bounds of a narrow uniformity is to enfeeble them. They naturally require wide and diversified modes of manifestation. And therefore it is wise that there should be in a Church no undue limitation as regards religious forms. Thus take the question of liturgies. That question has been endlessly debated on grounds which involve the rightness or wrongness of set forms of prayer on the one hand, and of what is termed *free* prayer on the other.

It has been contended on each side that it, and it alone, represents the lawful mode of worship in the Christian Church. The supporters of each view have brought forward copious evidence of what they consider fatal objections to the opposite practice. Now, the true conception of the matter seems to be that the worship of the Christian Church should combine *both* of these elements. Both of them are expressive of spiritual necessities. Each mode of prayer represents a natural utterance of devotional feeling. Those wants that are ever recurring, those intercessions which should be made day by day, and those confessions and thanksgivings which fall to be continually offered, find their appropriate expression in the use of identical language. To hold that each time we worship there should be an alteration of the terms in which the common subjects of prayer are referred to seems unreasonable and out of place. On the other hand, there are occasional and special themes which are frequently suggested, suggested often with great force, to the minds of a Christian congregation; a set form of worship cannot include *them*, and yet, unquestionably, they should enter into the devotions of the

Church. So that unprescribed prayer—prayer that originates in the circumstances of the time—would appear to be a not less fitting element of the services of the Christian Church than a liturgy. In the union of the two there is a fuller and richer provision for right worship than in possessing the one without the other.[1] It may be argued, indeed, that to permit liberty of deviating from a set form of prayer is a provision liable to be attended with abuse. But it has to be borne in mind that there is much less probability of such a consequence arising from the merely partial employment of this mode of devotion than there is from its use where no part of the public prayers is fixed. For, if those who conduct divine worship are accustomed to the use of a carefully-prepared and settled form, the effect must be so to guide their perception of what is fitting in devotional expression as to save them in great measure from mistakes when they are called upon to give utterance to prayer in language of their own.

[1] We have pointed out that Calvin and Knox both adopted this principle (pp. 86, 132). It was probably the intention of the Reformers generally that the two modes of prayer should be combined in public worship.

The principle which thus applies in the case of liturgies is one that may be wisely acted on in regard generally to the external matters of a Church,—the principle of maintaining as regards these the freedom and variety, which are needful to adapt them to the diversity of human wants. Traditionalism is an evil which finds ready nutriment in ecclesiastical soil. Forms and usages of the most rigid narrowness are often adhered to with obstinate zeal: not because they can be justified on the ground of utility, but merely because they belong to the past. Any proposal to enlarge the limits of religious liberty in this respect is frequently regarded with alarm. It is imagined that, by departing from rigid sameness of usage, a Church exposes itself to spiritual dangers of the most serious kind. We have sought, however, in what we have said in a preceding chapter, to show that the element of change must be taken into account as a condition which is inevitable in connection with the development of religious thought and feeling; and that, moreover, when wisely introduced and controlled, it exercises a beneficial influence. The worst corruptions of religion have been

A measure of liberty in regard to external matters necessary to healthy ecclesiastical life.

due, not to the introduction of alterations into the life and ordinances of the Christian Church, but to the absence of healthful reform. It is in the quiescence of religion, rather than in its changes, that error and spiritual declension have their origin. And, of all arguments that can be adduced against deviating from rigid tradition in the observances of a Church, that which seems most inconsistent is the danger of its leading to superstition. Such is the argument of those who believe that, by holding tenaciously and inflexibly to a severely simple, and even meagre, type of worship, we necessarily avoid the risk of falling into errors and corruptions of devotion. We have considered, in treating of sacerdotalism and puritanism, the merits of this argument. We have seen, as the result of comparing these two extremes of opinion, that there is no such safety from superstition in the maintenance of an austere rigour in religious observances as its advocates would have us suppose. What Bacon remarked in the Puritan asceticism of his time, —that there were the elements of superstition in it quite as truly as in the ceremonial system which it set itself to oppose—is still an important truth for the Christian Church. There is superstition in extravagant strictness as regards the external matters of religion, not less than in an excessive indulgence of ceremonial tendencies. The spiritual evil is the same in both cases. In the one extreme, as well as in the other, matters of mere form are magnified at the expense of religious life.

In this brief recapitulation of some of the principal points embraced in former parts of this work, we have hitherto referred only to subjects which belong to the *internal* nature and arrangements of the Christian Church. Some remarks will now be added on a topic, which has been also already alluded to, and which enters as an important element into ecclesiastical opinion, namely, the relations of the Church to human life in general, and to the affairs and duties of the world. *Relation of the Church to the life and work of the world.*

We say that this subject forms an important element in the views which are entertained in regard to church-matters: for the tone of ecclesiastical opinion largely depends on the idea that is held of the place the Church is designed to occupy in reference to ordinary human life. It *Tendency to separate the two.*

is, as we have seen in a previous chapter, a prevalent belief that the ecclesiastical sphere and that of the world are properly separate, and that the things which belong to the former have a character of higher sanctity than those pertaining to the latter. Some examples also have been given of the extent to which this belief has impressed itself on common thought, by referring to such distinctions as "sacred" and "secular," "spiritual" and "civil," "divine" service and "common" life. It is supposed by those who hold this view that the Church occupies a religious position superior to that of the everyday existence and engagements of man,—that within its precincts there is a diviner atmosphere than is to be found in the domain of ordinary activity. Ecclesiastical offices, and times, and places, and services are regarded as being on a higher level than the concerns of daily life. The solemnities of sacrament and pious ceremonial are looked on as involving a loftier degree of sanctity than can be attributed to the work of the world.

Such a separation inconsistent with New Testament teaching. Now, this idea of the relation of the Church to the world and to ordinary human life is radically untrue and unhealthy. It is altogether opposed to the representations of Christ and the New Testament writers. The view which they give of religion is, that its highest manifestation consists in the right discharge of our common obligations. The province of human action to which the New Testament assigns supreme importance is not that of ritual, but that of practice. Its idea of Christian service is not so much that which is associated with a material sanctuary, and set seasons and forms of worship, as " doing all things in the name of the Lord Jesus." It represents the whole of human life, and not merely a section of it, as sacred. All times, all places it regards as possessing a hallowed character to those who live as they ought. It is not in the offerings presented in a temple made with hands, and in acts of express devotion, that Christ or the Apostles describe the essential nature of Christianity as having its true expression; but in the life of pure thoughts and holy deeds. And the example of Jesus Christ himself, so far from having anything in common with the merely ecclesiastical type of sainthood, is the history of One who mingled in ordinary human concerns, who performed His share in the world's labour, and whose self-consecration was exhibited in the sorrows and cares of daily life.

The two disastrous effects of severing the Church from ordinary human life.

The separation of the sphere of the Church from that of the ordinary life of the world operates disastrously in two directions. In the first place, it inevitably leads to a depreciation of those everyday duties, which are by far the most important,—those duties which do not fall within the ecclesiastical pale, and yet are of the essence of Christian obligation. There are, it is true, devout natures which are so pure that, however excessive the veneration they devote to the ecclesiastical and ritual elements of religion, it is impossible for them to be otherwise than good in all the relations of life. But it is different with the great mass of professing Christians. The natural result in their case of the belief that religion is a business to be mainly transacted by means of special observances is to render them forgetful of the virtues of common existence. If the minute particulars of external ceremony receive supreme attention, it is at the expense of the essential obligations of life. The spirit of piety cannot be expended on points of ritual and matters of outward polity, without a corresponding neglect of practical goodness. And therefore it is always found that where fervour in regard to merely ecclesiastical subjects is most strong, and questions of religious form are allowed to assume pre-eminent importance, the charities and the moralities of life are suffered to decline. On the other hand, the severance of the domain of ordinary life from that of the Church has a not less disastrous influence on the Church itself. For that which most of all serves to give expansion of aim to a Christian society, and which tends most effectually to prevent the narrow feeling that is apt to affect it, is the influence of human life and human interests as a whole. The more of sympathy there is in a Church with the daily life of man, and the more it has of regard for the wants and aspirations of the world, the greater must be its freedom from fanatical feeling. The widening and bracing influences, that come to a religious communion through fellowship with the nature and necessities of mankind, are essential to its moral health. Deprived of these influences from without, and expending its spiritual energies within the contracted circle of its own existence, a religious society becomes infected with a false and morbid spirit. Its position of spiritual isolation is fatal to true and healthy life.

<small>This exemplified in the state of things existing during Christ's ministry.</small> There could not be a more forcible illustration of this fact than in the state of things which existed in connection with Christ's own ministry. The religious class with whom He was brought into contact claimed, above all things, a position of separateness from others.[1] They regarded the territory of orthodox belief and legal observances, which they occupied, as essentially apart from the common ground of worldly life. Within their own circle all sound faith and all true worship were, they imagined, to be found; outside it everything was unhallowed. Now, the verdict which the Saviour pronounced on the Pharisees, when He condemned their exclusiveness as false and bad—when He charged them with gross corruption, and declared that there was more of truth and righteousness in those who were outside their communion than there was among themselves—represents a fact of which there have been abundant instances in the history of

---

[1] The name Pharisees signifies the Separated.

religion. The tendency to make the life of piety that of a separate province from ordinary existence, and to keep it apart from the common life of the world, has often led to the most serious evils. It produces precisely those corruptions which it did in the case of the Pharisees. In proportion as religion recedes from the range of ordinary thought and life, and separates itself from common human interests, it loses the wholesome effects which are exercised by fellowship with what is broad and true ; and therefore readily becomes a prey to the evils of superstition and falseness which affected the Pharisaic character.

In the state of matters which existed in connection with the ministry of Christ we may thus recognize what is always one of the most formidable perils of the Christian Church. The true purpose of the Church is to act as a source of spiritual guidance to men in the duties of daily life. Its functions, instead of ending with the observances of worship, and the teaching of the sanctuary, have properly only their beginning there. The ultimate design of the existence of the Christian Church is to influence the entire

Daily existence the true sphere of the Church's influence.

range of human pursuits, and to impart a Christian character to the whole of human experience. It is really in the common business of men, and in their everyday engagements, that the true sphere of religion lies. The highest field for the exercise of Christian feeling is the work of the world, and not the performance of ritual acts. On the other hand, the belief is apt to find its way into a religious communion that the purpose of its existence is fulfilled when the routine of sacred service is gone through, and the requirements of ecclesiastical usage receive due attention. The relation of the Church of Christ to the interests and duties of ordinary life is thus too often lost sight of; religion degenerates into ecclesiasticism; it becomes mere church attendance, and exactness in regard to forms, and preciseness in doctrine, while the daily business of existence is hardly regarded as coming within its limits. While there is a continual danger to the Church arising from this tendency, it is impossible to over-estimate the seriousness of its results. Divorced from the thoughts and the wants of common life, ecclesiastical things are certain to yield to the influence of degeneracy and decay. It is in the living connection of a Church with the nature and necessities of men, that its fitness to fulfil its true vocation consists. And therefore there is the highest value in every provision that tends to make it a more effectual means of bringing Christianity to bear on the world at large; in everything which renders its services more accordant with the wants of human life, and its agencies better suited to the actual condition of things.

www.ingramcontent.com/pod-product-compliance
Lightning Source LLC
Chambersburg PA
CBHW030810230426
43667CB00008B/1155